M000213149

DENALI
Climbing Guide

0 11557 02717 4

DENALI
Climbing Guide

R. J. Secor

Maps by Mike Clelland
Drawings by Dee Molenaar

STACKPOLE
BOOKS

Copyright © 1998 by R. J. Secor

Published by
STACKPOLE BOOKS
5067 Ritter Road
Mechanicsburg, PA 17055

All rights reserved, including the right to reproduce this book or portions thereof in any form or by any means, electronic or mechanical, including photocopying, recording, or by any information storage and retrieval system, without permission in writing from the publisher. All inquiries should be addressed to Stackpole Books, 5067 Ritter Road, Mechanicsburg, PA 17055.

Printed in the United States

10 9 8 7 6 5 4 3 2 1

First edition

Cover design by Wendy Reynolds

IMPORTANT
The information regarding Denali National Park was accurate as of the publication of this book but is subject to change due to any number of factors. Readers are responsible for consulting park information centers in preparation for any trip to Denali.

Readers are also responsible for their own safety on Denali.The author and publisher of this book take no responsibility for any adverse outcomes incurred by mountaineers who use the information contained in *Denali Climbing Guide.*

Library of Congress Cataloging-in-Publication Data

Secor, R. J.
    Denali climbing guide / R. J. Secor. — 1st ed.
        p.   cm.
    Includes bibliographical references (p.) and index.
    ISBN 0-8117-2717-3 (pbk.)
    1. Mountaineering—Alaska—McKinley, Mount—Guidebooks.
    2. McKinley, Mount (Alaska)—Guidebooks. I. Title.
    GV199.42.A42M32555   1998   98-13262
                                                                             CIP

• CONTENTS •

• ACKNOWLEDGMENTS •

Art Freeman suggested many years ago that I write this book, but it took the strong encouragement of the late Malcolm Duff to persuade me to write the proposal and outline and to start the serious research needed for this book. I received a great deal of research assistance from Christi Burchard, librarian for The Mountaineers; Gretchen Lake and Marge Heath, University of Alaska; David R. Hirst, USGS Ice and Climate Project, University of Puget Sound; Joe McGregor and Nancy Papazian, USGS Photographic Library; Susan C. Eubank, Gay Ellen Roesch, and Virginia Boucher, American Alpine Club Library; and Cynthia Carey, Pasadena Public Library.

The text is supported by Dee Molenaar's outstanding sketches, and talented Mike Clelland drew the maps.

I especially want to thank the following individuals for sharing their route information, experiences, and genuine constructive criticism with me: Bob Rockwell, Larry Tidball, Gary Bocarde, Bill Hackett, Nancy Gordon, Michael Covington, Greg Collins, Neal Beidleman, Bob Schneider, Paul Fitzgerald, Steve House, Charles Raymond, James Wickwire, John Rehmer, Phil Powers, Alex Bertulis, my father John Secor, Eli Helmuth, Rudi Schmid, Greg Sievers, Michael Kennedy, Charley Shimanski, Rich Henke, Bob McGown, Ted Heckathorne, Dave Johnston, Walter Gonnason, Ian Wade, Stephen Koch, Lowell Thomas, Jr., Conrad Anker, Jeff Duenwald, Joe Davidson, Peter Reagan, Jed Williamson, Douglas Bingham, Bill Krause, Pete Metcalf, Glenn Randall, Ned Gillette, George Bell, Jr., Galen Rowell, James Given, Henry Florschutz, Shelly McGovern, Gus Benner, Michael Jenkins, Alan Eng, Bob Gammelin, Steve Swenson, Chris Jones, Tom Bennett, Julie Rush, James Wilson, Brian Okonek, Jim Okonek, Will Forsberg, and Daryl Miller. And I would be remiss if I didn't mention my Denali climbing partners, Tom Randel, Brian Smith, and Masaaki Hoshi.

I am grateful to Stackpole Books for publishing this book. The support I received from Judith Schnell, David Uhler, Larry Johnson, Dave Richwine, Jon Rounds, and Mark Allison has been outstanding.

R. J. Secor
Pasadena, California
May 1998

• INTRODUCTION •

I have written this book for experienced expedition mountaineers intent on climbing Denali, the highest mountain in North America. Well over a thousand climbers attempt Denali each year, and more than 80 percent take the Washburn Route. This has the reputation of being the easiest route, and just getting to the summit seems to be important to most climbers. I hope that experienced climbers will consider attempting other routes. I suspect that those who do so return to the real world with a satisfied imagination. It is important to be conservative when faced with objective dangers such as avalanches, hanging glaciers, and heavily crevassed glaciers, but those with many years of mountain experience and who are skilled in climbing difficult terrain should be more aggressive in selecting their routes.

The Northwest Buttress is a long, isolated route, but it offers a challenging climb leading to the beautiful summit of the North Peak. There are many ways to get to the long South Buttress, and climbing along this ridge is like being on the summit during the entire climb. The East Buttress is remote, and although parts of it are exposed to avalanches, the campsites are secure, and it offers intricate route-finding over difficult terrain. The Muldrow Glacier was the first route climbed on Denali, and it is still a true wilderness experience. Denali National Park and Preserve has strict prohibitions on the use of aircraft in the Denali Wilderness, so climbers must approach the north side of the mountain overland. Approaching Denali on snowshoes or skis with a dog team early in the season gives the expedition an ambience difficult to match in today's world.

There is no other mountain in the world like Denali. It is bigger than the great peaks of the Himalaya and the Karakoram Ranges. Mount Everest, for example, has a vertical rise of 12,000 feet from the Tibetan plateau, but

Denali is 18,000 feet above the Alaskan tundra. Mount Everest is approximately 4½° of latitude north of the tropic of Cancer, and Denali is 3½° south of the Arctic Circle. This far northern position makes Denali bitterly cold, and the atmosphere is thinner than that encountered at similar elevations in temperate or tropical latitudes. And Denali's proximity to the Aleutian Islands, "the birthplace of storms," gives it severe weather.

But most mountaineers who attempt Denali underestimate it. After all, almost five hundred "weekend warriors" climb to the top of the continent each year. Also, a 20,000-foot mountain is minor in the Andes and barely worth mentioning in the Himalaya or Karakoram. This misperception is reinforced by the mountaineering use fee charged by Denali National Park and Preserve, the visible presence of park personnel on the mountain, and the hundreds of climbers along the Washburn Route. But how do these things decrease the brutal effect that Denali's climate has on humans?

Many climbers believe that climbing Denali is necessary to gain experience before attempting the higher mountains in the Andes and the Himalaya. Although expedition experience on Denali is valuable for this goal, I believe that these climbers are wrong. In my view, expedition experience on high mountains in warmer, more benign climates is necessary before attempting Denali.

Denali is a tough peak, and in my opinion, it is a poor place to learn how to play the expedition game. Climbers who have minimal experience in expedition climbing should seriously consider taking advantage of the services of the commercial mountaineering guides who are permitted to operate in Denali National Park and Preserve. These guided expeditions are very safe, and the clients always learn a lot. Those who share their ambitions with the guide will learn even more and return from Denali with an excellent foundation to attempt the other great mountains of the world.

The "official" name of Denali is Mount McKinley, as determined by the ultimate authority on these matters, the United States Board of Geographic Names. But the State of Alaska Board of Geographic Names officially identifies it as Denali, the Athabaskan name for the mountain, meaning "The High One." Most Alaskans use Denali, as do most climbers who have visited its flanks. Mount McKinley National Park was officially renamed Denali National Park and Preserve in 1980 by the U.S. Congress under the Alaska National Interest Lands Conservation Act. But despite this act of Congress and decades of Alaskan public opinion, the United States Board of Geographic Names has resisted changing the name of the mountain.

The United States Board of Geographic Names does have a history of changing the name of the mountain, however. Those who look closely at the United States Geological Survey's 1:250,000 map, *Denali National Park and*

Preserve, or the 1:63,360 map, *Mt. McKinley (A-3), Alaska,* will see the name Churchill Peaks splashed across the two peaks that are atop the continent. These peaks were once officially named North Peak and South Peak by the United States Board of Geographic Names, but in 1965 they were renamed in honor of Sir Winston Churchill, apparently at the request of the National Park Service. The whole mountain is still called Mount McKinley, but the official name of the two principal summits is Churchill Peaks.[1]

Contrary to this bureaucratic view, the name Denali is used throughout this book, and Churchill Peaks will not be mentioned again. Other place names, created by the author, are Margaret Pass, Genet Basin, and Uemura Basin.

---

1. Donald J. Orth, *Dictionary of Alaska Place Names: Geological Survey Professional Paper 567* (Washington, DC: U.S. Government Printing Office, 1967), p. 219; and United States Board of Geographic Names, *Decisions on Geographic Names in the United States: October through December 1965,* Decision List no. 6504.

64°   152°   151°   150°   149°   64°

FAIRBANKS
90 miles

■ HEALY

DENALI
PARK
HEADQUARTERS ■

KANTISHNA
DENALI HIGHWAY
WONDER LAKE

TO PAXTON

DENALI
HIGHWAY
8

ALASKA RANGE

PETERS GLACIER
MULDROW GLACIER

RAVEN

63°   •DENALI   63°

GEORGE PARKS HIGHWAY

KAHILTNA GLACIER

TOKOSITNA GLACIER

RUTH GLACIER

Corvus corax

N

3

AREA
OF
DETAIL

ALASKA

•PETERSVILLE

GRIZZLY

TALKEETNA

Ursus arctos

ANCHORAGE
112 miles

0   10   20   30
MILES

62°   152°   151°   150°   149°

DENALI
NATIONAL PARK and PRESERVE

• CHAPTER I •

Preparations

ANCHORAGE

Most climbers enter Alaska by flying to Anchorage, the state's largest city. The cost of living can be reasonable for residents of the city but outrageous for visitors. Prices for rooms, restaurants, taxis, and other tourist-related services are high, but food prices in the supermarkets are only a little higher than those in major metropolitan cities in the lower forty-eight. Anchorage may be the last chance to visit a bank (the airport has automated teller machines and a currency exchange desk), and last-minute food and equipment purchases can be made at shopping centers in the city. There are no banks or supermarkets at either Talkeetna or Denali Park.

The most expeditious way to Talkeetna from Anchorage is to make a reservation with a shuttle service. The shuttle can meet climbers at the airport or a hotel, and brief stops can be made in Anchorage or Wasilla by making arrangements with the driver. The rates may vary with the number of passengers in the vehicle. Small groups can merge with others to get a better per-passenger rate.

The Alaska Railroad offers daily passenger service from Anchorage to Talkeetna and Denali Park starting in mid-May; there is only one northbound passenger train each Saturday before this date. The train fare may be less expensive than a shuttle, but one must factor in the cost of transportation from the airport to the railroad depot. The express train leaves Anchorage at 8:15 A.M., and the stop in Talkeetna (at 11:15 A.M.) is as short as possible. After making the mandatory check-in with the Mountaineering Rangers at the Talkeetna Ranger Station, those approaching Denali from the north may have to wait a day for the next northbound train to Denali Park.

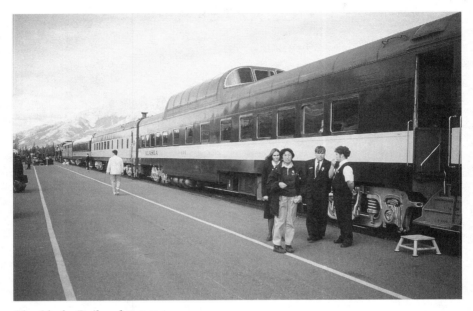

The Alaska Railroad. R. J. SECOR

TALKEETNA AND DENALI PARK

Talkeetna is approximately 115 miles north of Anchorage along George Parks Highway and Talkeetna Spur Road. It consists of about three hundred people and has dirt streets and log cabins, matching the popular imagination of what a small town in Alaska should look like. The residents extend warmth and welcome to visiting climbers, making Talkeetna a delightful place to prepare for a great climb. There are two small mountain shops for last-second equipment purchases. Overnight accommodations include a campground, some dormitories, and a couple of Alaskan roadhouses, as well as motels and bed-and-breakfast establishments. There are also a few restaurants, including a delicatessen serving pizza to famished climbers returning from the mountain. There may be a delay in flying to the mountain due to weather, and this time can be spent visiting the Talkeetna Historical Society Museum, housed in four restored buildings, including a railroad depot and a trapper's cabin. The old schoolhouse has an exhibit on Don Sheldon, the pioneer bush pilot who first landed climbers on Denali's glaciers on a commercial basis in the 1950s. The Section House features a 12-by-12-foot model of Denali surrounded by Bradford Washburn's oblique aerial photographs of the mountain. The saloon on the first floor of the historic Fairview Inn is also filled with entertaining historic memorabilia. And in the Talkeetna Cemetery is the Climbers' Memorial, listing the names of all the climbers who have died in the Alaska Range (contributions can be made to the Talkeetna Cemetery Association, P.O. Box 38, Talkeetna, AK 99676).

Denali Park is completely different. It is the main (and only motor vehicle) entrance to Denali National Park and Preserve. In July and August, it is crowded. The long lines at the Visitor Access Center consist of tourists seeking space in the campgrounds, backcountry permits, and shuttle-bus tickets. Denali Park is 238 miles north of Anchorage (or 138 miles north of Talkeetna Spur Road) along George Parks Highway. There is a large assortment of hotels, restaurants, private campgrounds, and stores outside of the park boundary (north of the road leading into Denali National Park and Preserve) to serve the needs of visitors who have been turned away when the campgrounds and the hotel in the park are full. Within the park boundary, Denali Park consists of a hotel with a restaurant and snack bar, a small store, a post office, a railroad station, a gravel airstrip, the national park headquarters, and two campgrounds. Riley Creek Campground is for recreational vehicles, and Morino Campground is a walk-in facility (no reservations are necessary). The latter will probably be preferred by most climbers, despite its proximity to the railroad tracks (freight trains run at night with distressing frequency).

Talkeetna ambience. R. J. SECOR

The shuttle buses that go as far as Wonder Lake usually start in mid-June. Tickets can be obtained at the Visitor Access Center at Denali Park and are available up to two days in advance. The buses serve not only tourists but also hikers and climbers, and there is a large seat-free area at the rear of each bus for packs and other gear. There are five buses each day, and the ride to Wonder Lake takes about six hours one way.

The mountaineering regulations require that all climbers check in in person at the Talkeetna Ranger Station, including those approaching the mountain from Wonder Lake. Instead of approaching Wonder Lake overland via Denali Park, many climbers now fly from Talkeetna to Kantishna and hike 9 miles to Wonder Lake. Another option, practical before the road opens, is to fly from Denali Park to Kantishna via bush plane.

CLIMBING REGISTRATION AND FEES

Even though the headquarters of Denali National Park and Preserve is located at Denali Park on the north side of the mountain, all mountaineering activities are managed from the National Park Service ranger station in Talkeetna. Registration forms and the authoritative booklet *Mountaineering: Denali National Park and Preserve* may be obtained from the Talkeetna Ranger Station (see appendix B).

It is mandatory that all expedition members attempting Denali (and Mount Foraker) preregister with the Denali National Park and Preserve at least sixty days before the start of their climb. Those who are not preregistered are prohibited from attempting Denali and Mount Foraker; there are no exceptions.

In addition to the preregistration requirement, Denali National Park and Preserve charges a mountaineering special-use fee of US$150 for each expedition member attempting Denali or Mount Foraker. *This is not rescue insurance.* The money is used by Denali National Park and Preserve to operate its mountaineering management program.

All expedition correspondence with the Talkeetna Ranger Station must be handled by one person—ideally, the leader. Each expedition must have its own name, which should be short and distinct. Each individual climber must complete a preregistration form identifying his or her significant previous climbs (hint: emphasize altitude), in addition to name, address, emergency notification, and so forth. The expedition leader collects all the registration forms into one package, encloses a nonrefundable and nontransferable deposit of US$25 for each expedition member, and sends it to the Talkeetna Ranger Station. Personal checks are not accepted, but Visa, MasterCard, or a money order made payable to "Denali National Park and

Preserve" is accepted. The balance of US$125 per climber (payable by credit card, money order, traveler's check, or U.S. currency) is due when the expedition checks in at the Talkeetna Ranger Station. One new member of the expedition may be added or substituted later. This new member must pay the deposit and submit the registration form at least thirty days before the start of the expedition.

All Denali and Mount Foraker expeditions must check in at the Talkeetna Ranger Station in person before the start of the climb, even those that plan to approach from the north. All climbers must show photographic identification. The Mountaineering Rangers will brief the climbers on the planned route, outline the conditions on the mountain, ensure that the party's equipment and supplies are adequate (by inquiry, not inspection), review safety and high-altitude medical information, and offer sincere, level-headed advice. Heed this orientation to Denali and subarctic mountaineering. The Mountaineering Rangers may wear nondescript uniforms, but they are all experienced Denali climbers, and it is foolish to ignore their counsel.

The last step is to check in again with the Talkeetna Ranger Station upon the completion of the expedition. Notes will be made on those who summited and/or reasons for failure, as well as accidents, injuries, or illnesses.

MAPS AND AERIAL PHOTOS

The best map of Denali is Bradford Washburn's *Mount McKinley, Alaska*. This 1:50,000 scale, shaded relief map (printed by the Swiss Federal Institute of Topography) is a work of art, showing the basins and ridges of Denali in detailed three dimension. It is available in the United States from the University of Alaska Press, P.O. Box 756240, University of Alaska–Fairbanks, Fairbanks, AK 99775-6240.

Although the Washburn map is beautiful, I have found the United States Geological Survey's 1:63,360 maps of Denali easier to read and use. (I would probably feel differently if I had started my topographic map reading career in Switzerland instead of the United States.) The west side of Denali is covered by *Talkeetna (D-3), Alaska* (File # AK 2579) and *Mt. McKinley (A-3), Alaska* (File # AK 1855), and the east side is covered by *Mt. McKinley (A-2), Alaska* (File # AK 1854) and *Talkeetna (D-2), Alaska* (File # AK 2578). Make sure that the "Talkeetna" maps are not "Talkeetna Mountains."

Mt. McKinley (B-2), Alaska (File # AK 1871) is needed for the approach to McGonagall Pass from Wonder Lake; in addition, *Mt. McKinley (B-3), Alaska* (File # AK 1870) is needed to approach Peters Glacier via Muddy River from Wonder Lake. Washburn also surveyed and published a map of the approach from Wonder Lake to McGonagall Pass. This is no longer in print, but it appeared as a supplement in the 1980 *American Alpine Journal.*

United States Geological Survey (USGS) topographic maps can be ordered from the USGS Branch of Distribution, Box 25286, Building 810, Denver Federal Center, Denver, CO 80225. It takes this agency a long time to fill orders, however, and it may be best to obtain both the USGS and the Washburn maps from map dealers. These maps can also be purchased in person at the Talkeetna Ranger Station and the Visitor Access Center at Denali Park.

Prints of Washburn's excellent oblique aerial photos of Denali (as well as the rest of the Alaska Range and Saint Elias Mountains) can be ordered from the University of Alaska–Fairbanks, P.O. Box 756808, Fairbanks, AK 99775-6806; telephone 907-474-6773.

CLIMB CLEAN

Denali receives a tremendous amount of human impact. Over one thousand climbers attempt the mountain each year, with more than 80 percent on the Washburn Route. Denali National Park and Preserve has a mandatory requirement that everything taken into the backcountry and the Denali Wilderness be taken out. Despite the law, a ton of trash has been removed from the Washburn Route in recent years.

The best way for climbers to limit their impact is to minimize what they carry onto the mountain. A party that brings surplus gear, food, and fuel to cover every imaginable contingency will have a much more difficult time removing the leftovers from Denali. Many well-intentioned (but naive) parties generously leave behind their surplus food and fuel at caches for other expeditions that may be in need of critical supplies. These caches are seldom used as intended, however, and end up as dumps high on the mountain. Climbers who deliberately abandon a cache will be cited by the Mountaineering Rangers. Give surplus food and fuel *in person* to another party, which will then either use it or pack it out. Best of all is not to carry it onto the mountain in the first place.

Another problem with caches is that they frequently disappear—not due to pilfering by other climbers, but due to ravens and heavy snowfall. Food, fuel, and equipment that has been relayed to a higher campsite (or left behind at a lower campsite for later retrieval) must be well buried and well marked. Bury the cache at least 3 feet deep, preferably under large snow blocks. Mark the cache with two or three wands that have been taped together, or better yet, mark it with a 6-foot pole topped by a wand. (Some experienced Denali climbers also mark it with an avalanche beacon.) Label

Climbers on Motorcycle Hill, Washburn Route. R. J. Secor

both the buried cache and the wand with the expedition name and the expected date of return. In fact, it is wise to mark *everything* with the climber's *and* expedition's names. Many times, lost or misplaced equipment is returned to the owner through the climbers' grapevine.

Digging up the "Eleven Foot Cache" at 11,000 feet, Washburn Route. R. J. SECOR

A party should carry a maximum of twenty-five days of food and fuel on the Washburn Route, and thirty-five days of supplies on the Muldrow Glacier or any other route that is approached from the north. As a rough guideline, figure a maximum of 2 pounds of food per person per day and 0.25 quart of white gas or kerosene per person per day.[1] For example, a party of four bound for the Washburn Route with 360 pounds of food and 60 quarts (15 gallons) of fuel is probably carrying too much. For this party, 200 pounds of food and 24 quarts (6 gallons) of fuel should be plenty.

Another way to minimize impact is to repackage all food into plastic bags. Bulky store packaging can add 25 percent to the net weight of food; for a climber, this packaging is dead weight that must be carried not only up the mountain but also down and out. It is much more efficient to repackage all foodstuffs into plastic bags. When the food has been consumed, it is easy to

---

1. Experienced climbers may believe that this amount of stove fuel is excessive, but the cold temperatures and dry snow on Denali require that more fuel be burned to melt snow for an equivalent amount of water than on other high mountains. Winter climbers on Denali allow 0.5 quart of fuel per person per day.

collapse the bags into compact bundles and carry them down the mountain. Paper and cardboard can be burned, but it is messy, and the resulting piles of ash mark the snow with sooty patches, much like the handholds of classic rock climbs are marked by patches of chalk. It is far more efficient, and more environmentally sound, to use plastic bags and carry them out instead of burning paper.

There may be more than two hundred climbers camped at Genet Basin in June of each year, and Denali National Park and Preserve has wisely installed a pit latrine there. It must be used for both feces and urine. At campsites that lack latrines, defecate directly into a biodegradable bag, tie it shut, and dump it into a crevasse. Only human waste may be deposited into crevasses, never trash. And every expedition member should urinate at the same spot at each campsite. This can be marked by a wand.

Abandoned fixed ropes on technical routes have become a serious conservation and safety problem on Denali. At one time there were twelve separate fixed ropes in the Japanese Couloir on Cassin Ridge. One climber fell to his death in 1974 trusting an ancient fixed line. Aside from the fixed ropes on the headwall of the Washburn Route (which are seasonally maintained by the guide concessionaires), all fixed ropes must be removed.

An attempt on Denali involves a considerable investment of time and money. The goal of every climber is to return home safely from the summit. There is no reason why these climbers cannot also make the commitment to leave the mountain clean. There is far less effort involved in removing one's own rubbish from the mountain than there is in reaching the summit. With proper planning and organization, it is not only possible but also easy to minimize each climber's impact on the mountain. All of us must make the commitment to leave Denali clean.

CLIMB SMART

Mountaineering is inherently dangerous, and the danger in climbing Denali is magnified due to its remoteness, weather, altitude, and glaciers. This danger will always be present, but there are many things that can be done to reduce the risks.

What follows may sound like a tedious, finger-shaking lecture. An expedition to Denali is not a matter of right or wrong; instead, it is a series of decisions, and each decision has many consequences. No one is immune from disaster, but with a realistic assessment of the hazards and an honest appraisal of the skills, strengths, and weaknesses of the party, climbers can significantly reduce the risks by making the correct choices.

Helicopter landing at Genet Basin. R. J. SECOR

ATTITUDE

This is most important: all expeditions must be self-sufficient, and all decisions must be based on maintaining the expedition's self-sufficiency. This means that an expedition cannot rely on anyone else for assistance in the event of an emergency. Plan your climb with the commitment to be self-sufficient, and climb only by maintaining your group's self-sufficiency. Everything else (including the summit) is secondary.

Many climbers have (or had) the deadly misperception that the hundreds of other climbers along the Washburn Route and the visible presence of personnel from Denali National Park and Preserve provide an implicit safety net. This false assumption is reinforced by the mountaineering special-use fee, the ranger camp at Genet Basin, and the helicopters that seem to make routine flights between Talkeetna and the ranger camp at 14,200 feet on Denali.

The mountaineering special-use fee is collected by Denali National Park and Preserve to cover the costs of operating its mountaineering program; it is not rescue insurance. The ranger camp at 14,200 feet is there to assist climbers in the early detection of altitude sickness, to coordinate rescues performed by acclimatized personnel, to improve the on-site evaluation of rescue capability, to provide better communications between Denali and Talkeetna, and to prevent premature or unnecessary rescues. In other words, the special-use fee, the ranger camp, and the helicopter are for the people *doing* the rescues. Think of the fee as a tax, and the ranger camp as a fire station. No logical person believes that taxes have a direct benefit to an individual taxpayer or would ignore a fire hazard in his or her home because of the existence of a fire department. But this is the laughable logic that many climbers have on Denali.

Moreover, one cannot expect a rescue to happen immediately upon request. Let's say that there is an emergency high on the mountain and that Denali National Park and Preserve personnel have determined that a rescue is necessary. Are acclimatized rescuers available? Will the weather allow the helicopter to hover or land at the accident site? These two big questions are just the beginning of a series of decisions that must be made on the mountain and in Talkeetna by many people before an effective rescue can be attempted. It might be a long time before rescue personnel arrive at the scene, and a self-sufficient party could make a big difference in the outcome of the situation.

Another common mistake is reliance on other expeditions. For example, parties have started up Denali with inadequate supplies, expecting to live off surplus food and fuel carried by descending expeditions. Or a party may observe another expedition moving on the mountain and follow it, assuming that the first party knows what it is doing, where it is going, and what is happening. Many people go through life relying on the kindness of strangers, but it is a hell of a way to climb Denali.

The best way to maintain an expedition's self-sufficiency is to keep the party together. This is especially important today, because most expeditions consist of only three to four climbers. It goes without saying that a divided party is weaker. Low on the mountain, a segment of an expedition may be unable to carry out a successful crevasse rescue by itself. Individuals have different rates of acclimatization, and well-acclimatized (but impatient) climbers may be tempted to move to a higher camp and ultimately the summit, leaving their companions behind to make their own attempt later. It frequently happens that essential equipment (a working stove, adequate food and fuel, or a shovel) is missing from one of these campsites, with disastrous consequences. Most parties separate because the members are too focused on the summit. Instead of aiming for the summit, the primary goal should be to get everyone off the mountain with no injuries or illnesses after climbing as high on the mountain as possible. The objective should be to get everyone to the high camp well acclimatized, well fed, well hydrated, and with adequate equipment and supplies. Only after this is accomplished can the secondary goal (the summit) be attempted and attained. After all, the summit of Denali is the icing on the cake.

ALTITUDE

The high altitude is the most common cause of illness on Denali, and most accidents with injuries occur above 14,000 feet. Those who have climbed 20,000-foot (or higher) peaks in the other great ranges of the world may dismiss Denali's altitude as an insignificant factor. But the earth's atmosphere is thinner at the poles than at the equator, and the 20,320-foot South Summit of Denali, at 63° 04' 10" north latitude, has a barometric pressure equivalent to 21,700 feet, in theory. In reality, the barometer at 14,200 feet consistently reads just above a half atmosphere; theoretically, a half atmosphere is at 18,000 feet at 30° north, the latitude of the Himalaya. Also, there are tremendous barometric pressure variations on a daily basis at 14,200 feet, equal to 500 feet of altitude gain or loss, and these variations are magnified during bad weather. Himalayan veterans have reported that they felt as if they were at 22,000 to 24,000 feet on the summit.

Climbers should be familiar with the following mountain illnesses:

Acute Mountain Sickness (AMS). AMS occurs after too rapid an ascent to 6,000 to 7,000 feet. Headache, dizziness, drowsiness, shortness of breath, nausea, and sometimes vomiting are the classic symptoms. The best cure is rest and descent to a lower elevation. At a lower altitude, the illness usually subsides fairly quickly, and the climb can be resumed after a day or two of rest.

High-Altitude Pulmonary Edema (HAPE). HAPE is a serious, life-threatening medical emergency. It comes on rapidly and has been known to cause death less than forty hours after a rapid climb to 10,000 feet. One subjective warning is to observe who is the most fit at the start of the expedition. If that person's fitness decreases as he or she climbs higher on the mountain, that individual may contract HAPE. Another warning is extreme weakness going uphill. HAPE is affected by cold, so keep yourself as warm as possible. The symptoms include a cough with bloody or foamy sputum, shortness of breath, general weakness, and a gurgling sound in the chest. If any of these symptoms appear, assume the worst and get the victim to a lower elevation as soon as possible. An authority on this illness, Dr. Charles S. Houston, has noted: "High altitude pulmonary edema may proceed rapidly to coma and death, or may improve with equal speed if the victim goes down only a few thousand feet after symptoms begin."[2] If the victim can't move, carry him or her to a lower elevation. If oxygen is available, administer it. Some expeditions may have a portable hyperbaric chamber (such as the Gamow Bag). This increases the barometric pressure around the

---

2. Charles S. Houston, M.D., "Altitude Illness—Recent Advances in Knowledge," *American Alpine Journal* 22, no. 1 (1979): 155.

victim, simulating a lower altitude. This is no substitute for descent, but it may be useful for treatment when descent is impossible due to weather or terrain.

High-Altitude Cerebral Edema (HACE). HACE is not common (I have seen only one case of it), but it is the most serious of the mountain illnesses. Symptoms include a severe headache, staggering, and hallucinations, possibly leading to coma and death. It rarely occurs below 14,000 feet. As with pulmonary edema, carry the victim (if necessary) to a lower elevation to save his or her life.

The best medicine for all of these ailments is prevention, and there are some things that climbers can do to minimize their risk of illness and improve their performance.

Ascend Slowly. The mountaineer's dictum "climb high, sleep low" is the best method to prevent altitude sickness. The crucial factor is the *sleeping* altitude. Dr. Peter Hackett recommends, "Once above 3,000 meters (9,842 feet), limit your net gain in altitude (your sleep altitude) to 300 meters per day (1,000 feet)."[3] The climb from Kahiltna Base to Genet Basin at 14,200 feet should not be done in less than five days, and even this may be too fast for some team members. Most expeditions take eight days. At least a couple of rest days should be taken at 14,200 feet; this time is usually spent fortifying the campsite and building igloos for protection from storms.

Many climbers attempt Denali with only two weeks of vacation time and climb too fast. This is not enough time to climb Denali even under ideal conditions (which are rare). Those coming from Europe or Asia may need a total of seven days just to travel to Talkeetna, fly to the mountain, and return home.

Drink Water. Although dehydration does not cause mountain sickness, it decreases physical performance and the ability to generate heat from muscles, contributing to chilling and fatigue, which may lead to HAPE as well as hypothermia and frostbite. Four quarts per day is the minimum, and 6 quarts is not too much. Think of water as a harmless recreational drug. I believe that it transforms my personality, making me more relaxed, more alert, and more attractive to members of the opposite sex.

Don't Push Yourself. Racing up Denali each day is a good way to bring on mountain sickness. Those who are young and fit are more susceptible to AMS, HAPE, and HACE simply because they climb faster and therefore are more prone to fatigue and chilling. A slow, steady pace will serve you better than the "dash and crash" that seems to be the norm.

---

3. Peter H. Hackett, M.D., *Mountain Sickness: Prevention, Recognition, and Treatment* (New York: American Alpine Club, 1980), p. 60.

Don't Drink Alcohol. Even small amounts of alcohol seem to be detrimental to good acclimatization, in my experience. There is also some anecdotal evidence that alcohol may be a contributing factor to HACE.

Drugs. Many climbers take medication on the advice of their physicians to prevent or relieve the major symptoms of acute mountain sickness.[4] My two "drugs" of choice are water and descent. If I have a headache at altitude, I drink a quart of water. The headache is usually gone by the time I finish the quart. If I still have a headache an hour later, I drink another quart while descending.

FROSTBITE

Altitude is the most common cause of illness, but frostbite is the most common injury. Getting frostbite is failure (there is no cure for it) and I believe that most climbers who get it leave the mountain without mentioning it in their postclimb reports. Frostbite is prevented not just by wearing warm clothing but also by proper body maintenance. Being well fed, well hydrated, and well acclimatized are much more important than wearing and using state-of-the-art clothing and equipment. Supergaiters (which leave the boot sole exposed) won't make it on Denali; complete, insulated overboots are mandatory. Inside the overboots, wear the best oversized double boots that you can afford (the closed-cell foam inner boots may expand at altitude), plus a set of thick socks with an extra insole and a vapor barrier sock. Many climbers carry a special set of Summit Socks, which are not worn until the summit day.

As a general rule, if one's feet or hands haven't warmed up after an hour of climbing, expect frostbite. The symptoms start with cold feet and/or hands and progress to pain. The pain is a warning sign to rewarm the extremity immediately. (Those who ignore the pain may suddenly feel "warm" hands and feet; in reality, their extremities have gone numb, and they have deep frostbite.) Rewarming is most easily done by placing the hands in someone's armpits or placing the bare feet on someone's stomach until they feel warm. Don't hesitate to ask your partners for this service, and don't hesitate to offer it to a victim. If this doesn't work, turn back. The summit of Denali is not worth frostbite.

It is too late to use this method to rewarm deep frostbite, marked by pale white skin that is ice hard. In this case, the best treatment is to keep the hand or foot frozen until rapid rewarming of the frozen extremity can be done in a warm (100° F to 108° F) bath. This must be done in a place where

---

4. Colin Kerst Grissom, M.D., "Medical Therapy of High Altitude Illness," *American Alpine Journal* 35 (1993): 118–23.

the victim's entire body can be kept warm during and after treatment and where the victim can be easily evacuated without walking on his or her feet. This is a painful treatment, and after rewarming, the victim must be carried to prevent further damage. Frostbite must be avoided at all costs, including the summit.

CLIMBING FALLS

Falling off a mountain matches the popular imagination of the big danger in mountaineering, and this is the most common accident on Denali. The Orient Express—a tactless, macabre name—is most famous for its climbing falls, but more climbers have fallen on the "Autobahn," the traverse between 17,200 feet and Denali Pass along the Washburn Route, than on any other route on Denali. The first climbing fall here occurred in 1960 when Jim Whittaker fell and pulled off his three rope partners after making a rapid (only three days from 10,200 feet) climb to the summit. Undoubtedly, exhaustion and no acclimatization contributed to this accident, but the big error was the failure to place protection (pickets, snow flukes, or some other buried anchor) between the climbers.[5] This type of accident and its causes have been repeated with distressing frequency on Denali. Another important contributing factor is the use of ski poles instead of ice axes. Stopping a falling climber with an ice axe self-arrest is a plucky act at best, but to do so with ski poles is hopeless.

CREVASSE FALLS

Guide Gary Bocarde describes Peters Basin as "a very holy glacier and I mean very, very holy!" In other words, there are lots of holes, or crevasses. The crevasses on Denali are huge and deceptive. Most falls into crevasses are bad, with the victim hanging free from a rope deeply embedded in the edge of an overhanging lip. Crevasses can easily be 60 to 100 feet wide, bridged by winter's weak, cold, light wind-slab snow and unmarked by the sagging surface that identifies hidden crevasses in other ranges. As the season progresses, the many hours of daylight create wet, slushy snow conditions, and the snow that typically falls in June and July does not appreciably strengthen the few remaining bridges. It is best to travel during the early morning hours low on the mountain in the late season. Climbers should remain roped together with taut ropes and be well separated during rest stops so that if someone falls into a crevasse it will be only one member, not

---

5. To be fair, I should state that placing protection between roped climbers on steep snow slopes was not a common practice among American mountaineers in the early 1960s.

A well-spaced rest on Kahiltna Glacier. R. J. SECOR

the whole party. Sleds should be attached to the pack (not directly to the climber) and the climbing rope so that the load can be jettisoned by a fallen climber. Campsites must be well probed by the rope leader before the other climbers approach, unrope, and set up camp. And any climber who leaves the probed area must be belayed.

I believe that most climbers have no idea of how difficult it can be to haul someone out of a crevasse. Theoretically, a C x Z pulley system has a 6:1 mechanical advantage: 1 pound of pulling force should raise 6 pounds of the victim's weight. In theory, a rescuer would have to exert only 33 pounds of force to raise a 200-pound victim. In reality, friction in even the most efficient C x Z pulley system reduces the mechanical advantage to 2.5:1. The rescuer would have to exert 80 pounds of pulling force to raise a 200-pound victim in the real world.[6]

Rescuing someone from a crevasse is not easy, it cannot be learned from a book, and no one can afford to forget about it until needed. Crevasse rescue is not the most glamorous technique in mountaineering, but all members of the expedition must practice it realistically. Lacking a real crevasse, throw an old rope over the limb of a tree or from the edge of a balcony or bridge, tie 200 pounds (the weight of 24 gallons of water) to its end, and learn how much

6. Bruce Hendricks, "An Ace in the Hole: A Look at Some Recent Research on Crevasse Rescue Systems," *Canadian Alpine Journal* (1991): 92-95.

strength is really needed to raise this mass to salvation. It is especially important for parties composed of only two climbers to practice this again and again before attempting Denali.

RESCUE

If an expedition cannot handle its own emergency after an honest assessment of the situation and the resources at hand, it should first seek assistance from other nearby climbers. This demands caution, however, because the skill and strength of another expedition may not be equal to the demands of the crisis, and climbers from different countries may not speak a common language. All mountaineers should give aid to those in need, but unfortunately, this is not always as forthcoming as desired, due to "summit fever" and a lack of compassion. When all else fails, it is time to call for additional help via the radio.

The preferred radio is a 3- to 5-watt handheld transceiver with a citizens band (CB) channel 19 (27.185 MHz) crystal.[7] This frequency is monitored by Denali National Park and Preserve in Talkeetna and at the 14,200-foot ranger camp along the Washburn Route. The glacier pilots also monitor this frequency while flying, as does the Kahiltna Base camp manager, who broadcasts daily mountain weather forecasts. Those on the north side of Denali will also need a CB channel 7 (27.035 MHz) crystal. This channel is monitored by resorts at Kantishna beginning in mid-May.

The citizens band frequency is line of sight, and it may be necessary to move to another location (perhaps only a few yards) to reach a base station. Or another expedition may receive the message and relay it to the rangers. In any case, the message should be brief and specific: the name of the expedition, the nature of the emergency, the weather at the scene, the exact location and elevation, the number of climbers who can assist, and the party's immediate plans.

It can be argued that a radio makes an expedition less self-sufficient. Denali National Park and Preserve encourages all parties to carry a radio, however, because it minimizes miscommunications during a rescue. If the mountaineering use fee is thought of as a tax and the ranger camp is thought of as a fire station, then think of the radio as a personal self-defense weapon. The key to carrying pepper spray, chemical mace, or even a firearm is to use common sense so that the weapon is used only as a last resort. Radios are also the best way to remain part of the grapevine, keeping everyone informed of what is happening on the mountain.

---

7. Some radios have a forty-channel capacity. Radios with only one to three channels (crystals) are more reliable in the cold, however. It is wise to install two channel 19 crystals in such radios. All radios and batteries must be warmed before use.

SEASONS AND WEATHER

The climbing season on Denali is from April through July. Generally, the early season (April and May) has less precipitation, but it is much colder, with fierce winds from the north typically occurring with clear skies. Crevasses are thinly bridged, and the upper part of Denali is usually covered with hard snow. Climbing conditions may be better in the early season, but the weather can be ferocious. June and July (late season) are warmer, but there are more clouds, more precipitation, and fewer bridges across crevasses, and deep, new snow can impede travel. It is interesting to note that those who have climbed the sharp ridges on the south, southeast, and east sides of Denali have reported fewer problems with cornices and avalanches on the lower part of the mountain (below 14,000 feet) in the early season than in the late season. Denali's best climbing weather is in July, when the weather on the upper part of the mountain is mildest and more stable, and low-level clouds may blanket the land surrounding the mountain. Most climbers are on the mountain from the middle of June to the middle of July.

It never becomes truly dark during the climbing season. There are seven hours of darkness at sea level in early April at 63° north (four and a half hours in mid-April, and two hours in late April). Denali's great height lengthens the period of twilight, making it feasible to climb at all hours without head-

Tent and windbreak before a five-day storm. R. J. SECOR

lamps. In fact, it is theoretically possible to see the sun at midnight on the summer solstice from Denali's summit. Although Denali is 179 statute miles south of the Arctic Circle, the mountain's great altitude, combined with atmospheric refraction (amplified by nonstandard conditions of subzero temperatures and low air pressure) and the ellipsoid shape of the earth, makes the sun's image appear higher. In other words, it may be possible to see the sun *on the other side of the earth* from the summit of Denali at the solar low point (approximately 2:00 A.M. Alaska Daylight Savings Time) on the summer solstice.

Bad weather is normal. The best strategy is to move the party slowly low on the mountain (below 14,000 feet), even during poor or bad weather. Climb and descend expeditiously while high (above 14,000 feet) on Denali when the weather is good, and carry a week's worth of food and fuel in case the weather goes back to being normal. The weather rules above 14,000 feet on Denali.

The big storms on Denali originate in the Aleutians. The Pacific High, north of Hawaii, may move northward into the Gulf of Alaska, forcing Aleutian storms to move to the northeast across the interior of Alaska instead of to the east across the northern Pacific Ocean. Denali, the biggest mountain in the Alaska Range (arguably, the biggest mountain in the world), receives the brunt of these storms moving out of the southwest.

Tent and windbreak after a five-day storm. R. J. SECOR

Igloo before a five-day storm. R. J. Secor

But these storms are relatively easy to predict. The first and most important indicator is the air temperature. Overnight (or perhaps I should say twilight) temperatures are typically far below 0° F during good, clear weather high on the mountain. Bad weather brings warmer temperatures, close to 0° F and perhaps a bit higher. This is usually followed by a ring around the sun or moon (twenty-four hours before the storm), then high cirrus clouds ("mares' tails") and increasing winds (twelve hours before the storm). When the storm hits, expect hurricane-force winds (80 to 100 miles per hour or greater) with heavy snowfall for the next week. All camps, especially those at or above 14,000 feet, must be dug in well, with massive snow windbreaks completely surrounding tents, and igloos available in the event of tent failure. This is no exaggeration. Expect to get slam-dunked by a Denali storm.

Never underestimate the potential force or length of a storm on Denali. Let's say that an expedition is at a high camp and ready to go for the summit and the morning brings cirrus clouds with relatively warm temperatures. Forsake the summit, break camp, and move it to a more sheltered location lower on the mountain before the storm arrives. After five to seven days of intense, stressful weather at or above 17,000 feet, the party may not have the strength to descend, let alone summit.

Remember that good weather on Denali means cold temperatures. It is

Igloo after a five-day storm. R. J. SECOR

not uncommon for parties to start for the summit in good weather with air temperatures of –20° F to –30° F, perhaps warming as high as 0° F as the day progresses.

Another weather phenomenon is the lenticular cloudcap. This occurs when moist wind from the ocean strikes the upper part of the mountain, where it is forced upward, cools, and condenses, creating fog, winds, and/or snow near the summit; the larger area surrounding Denali may be completely clear. Typically, this occurs suddenly in the afternoon and gradually dissipates with colder temperatures as the sun dips lower in the sky in the evening. Please don't conclude that I am suggesting that mountaineers should climb into the cloudcap and expect it to disappear upon their arrival at the summit. Conditions within the cloudcap can be intense, and anyone who climbs into it is risking his or her life.

Watch the weather every day during the climb. Make written notes on the overnight temperatures, changes in the altimeter, winds, and clouds. Note the time of day that lenticular clouds appear on Mount Foraker or Denali, estimate the altitude of their lower edges, and note when they disappear. After all this study, one should have a good understanding of the weather pattern on Denali by the time of the summit dash.

This discussion of predicting the weather may not seem necessary,

Lenticular cloud on Mount Foraker. R. J. SECOR

because official weather forecasts are broadcast daily by the Kahiltna Base camp manager and repeated by personnel at the ranger camp at Genet Basin. Once, however, the camp manager and the park rangers did not receive an official weather forecast. At the appointed hour, a Denali National Park and Preserve mountaineering volunteer gave what appeared to be an official forecast over the radio, based on his own intelligent weather observations during his past two weeks on Denali. And it was very accurate, of course!

AIRPLANES AND DOGS

There are eight air taxis that serve Denali climbers. These businesses are listed in appendix B. Contact them for information on their latest rates, deposit requirements, and services offered. Their prices for round-trip flights between Talkeetna and Kahiltna Base or Ruth Glacier are more or less the same, but their prices for other services vary greatly. These other services may include air or ground transportation between Anchorage and Talkeetna and overnight accommodations and secure storage facilities in Talkeetna. In addition, maps, white gas, and wands may be purchased, and CB radios, snowshoes, and sleds may be available for rental.

The aircraft can carry up to three climbers and their gear. Those flying to Kahiltna Base receive a base-camp card from the flight service, listing the name of the expedition, the number of sleds rented, and the amount of white gas purchased. This is given to the Kahiltna Base camp manager, an individual seasonally employed by all the Talkeetna air taxis offering glacier landings. The camp manager gives the expedition its sleds and fuel and points out the cache site (leave five days of food here) and campsites. At the end of the climb, check in with the camp manager. He or she will call the air taxi, tell it that you are ready to be flown out, and give it a report on current weather conditions. You might fly out with a different air taxi from the one that flew you in.

The sleds available from the flight services are simple, inexpensive, plastic children's sleds, such as those used at snow play areas. (Some climbers have gone to great expense and brought to Alaska sleds specifically designed for cross-country ski tours, only to find that they don't fit inside an airplane.) The sleds may come with traces and enough cord to lash the load securely, but play it safe and bring your own. The V-shaped traces should be at least as long as the climber is tall. Tie a piece of webbing around your pack, and attach the traces to this with a locking carabiner. Bring an extra prusik sling to attach the end of the sled to the climbing rope.

Aircraft landings and airdrops are prohibited within the Denali Wilderness. Horse and mule packing is also prohibited, and sled dogs are allowed on Denali only with the superintendent's permission. There is a commercial

Loading the airplane in Talkeetna. R. J. SECOR

dog sled freighting service that operates on the north side of Denali. The expedition's food is packed into wooden crates or 5-gallon buckets and shipped to a Talkeetna air service. The provisions are then flown to Kantishna, where they are picked up by the dog team and cached during early spring to be picked up later during the climb. Stove fuel can also be ordered from the air service and cached. The empty wooden boxes, plastic buckets, fuel cans and other items used by the expedition must be thoroughly burned or carried out by the climbers. The address is listed in appendix B.

HOW TO USE THIS BOOK

The routes are presented in counterclockwise order, starting with the Traleika Spur on the northeast side of Denali. The words "left" and "right" in the route descriptions are given from the perspective of facing the summit that each route ends atop. To avoid confusion, a cardinal direction is also offered, such as "left (northwest)."

The routes have been rated in terms of overall difficulty using Boyd Everett's Alaska Grade System.[8] This system of grading climbs in Alaska and the Yukon is based on the length of the route, the amount of technical climbing, the altitude of the technical difficulties, and exposure to objective dangers. The length of the approach has no bearing on the rating.

Alaska Grade 1 is a simple route that can be completed in a day on a low mountain in Alaska or the Yukon. Needless to say, there are no Alaska Grade 1 routes on Denali.

Alaska Grade 2 is a more difficult climb on a low mountain or an "easy" (nontechnical) route on a high mountain. One of the principles of the Alaska Grade System is that high-altitude routes (above 17,000 feet) are rated one grade higher than comparable routes on a lower mountain, due to the problems of cold and altitude. Muldrow Glacier and the Washburn Route are Alaska Grade 2.

Alaska Grade 3 is a route with few, minimal technical difficulties, typically no higher than Yosemite Decimal System (YDS) class 4. The Thayer Route on the South Buttress and the East Buttress Route are Alaska Grade 3.

Alaska Grade 4 is a route with sustained, difficult climbing. Reality Rib and West Rib are examples of Alaska Grade 4.

Alaska Grade 5 features extended stretches of hard to extreme climbing on a long route. Cassin Ridge is Alaska Grade 5.

Alaska Grade 6 has all the qualifications of an Alaska Grade 5, but the

---

8. Boyd N. Everett, Jr., *The Organization of an Alaskan Expedition* (Pasadena, CA: Gorak Books, 1984), pp. 87-88.

route must be huge, with prolonged stretches of severe climbing. In Everett's opinion, the only Alaska Grade 6 routes were the gigantic ridges on the southern side of Mount Logan in the Yukon. Hummingbird Ridge on Mount Logan, for example, is 6 miles long and gains more than 14,000 feet along a continuous sharp, exposed ridge. In contrast, Cassin Ridge on Denali gains 9,000 feet in 2 miles.

Everett created the Alaska Grade System in 1966, and over the years, grade inflation has occurred. This is the bane of the guidebook author. How can one write a route description that is accurate and current without adding more (and implicitly approving of) grade inflation?

The difficulty of the individual pitches of technical routes has been rated using either the Union Internationale des Associations d'Alpinisme (UIAA) System or the YDS. The UIAA System has been in existence since the 1960s, but it wasn't until 1989 that the UIAA actually created a table that compared the UIAA System with the YDS as well as with the French, British, Australian, and German systems. In 1995, this table was revised (and it also compared the UIAA System with the Polish, Swedish, Romanian, Danish, Ukrainian, Finnish, South African, and Kurghizsean systems). Instead of listing both ratings, which may not match in reality, one or the other has been noted, with the assumption that whoever reported it was probably familiar with his or her own native system.

What follows is the 1995 comparison of the YDS and the UIAA System. Again, there is no guarantee that these grades will actually match in the real world.

YDS	UIAA
5.4	I
5.5	II
5.6	III
5.7	IV
5.8	V- to V
5.9	V+ to VI-

The most important way to use this book is as a start for research. Each route description is just that, a description, but it is followed by references. A savvy mountaineer will seek these out, study them, and learn about the logistical problems, climbing strategies, and weather experienced by previous parties. After reading all available reference material, contact the climbers who have climbed or attempted these routes to learn more. One advantage of the bureaucracy of the Denali National Park and Preserve is that there are excellent records of who did what, when, where, and how. (They haven't quite mastered the why, however.) Find out as much information about the proposed route as possible. The following abbreviations are used for the references cited:

- *AAJ: American Alpine Journal,* published annually by the American Alpine Club, 710 Tenth Street, Suite 140, Golden, CO 80401.

- *ANAM: Accidents in North American Mountaineering,* published annually by the American Alpine Club, 710 Tenth Street, Suite 100, Golden, CO 80401.

- *CAJ: Canadian Alpine Journal,* published annually by the Alpine Club of Canada, Box 1026, Banff, Alberta, T0L 0C0, Canada.

• CHAPTER 2 •

Northern Routes

Airplane landings and airdrops are prohibited within the Denali Wilderness, so these routes are approached overland from Wonder Lake, located approximately 85 miles from Denali Park by a good dirt road. The road to Wonder Lake is closed to private vehicles, and climbers usually take the shuttle buses that run between the park headquarters and Wonder Lake, when the road is passable during the summer. The road is usually open by mid-June each year, and the six-hour bus ride includes many impromptu stops to view wildlife. When the road is closed in the early season, climbers either approach Wonder Lake by ski and dog sled from Denali Park or fly to Kantishna (a village just outside the Denali Wilderness boundary that is almost as far north from Denali as Talkeetna is south) and hike, snowshoe, or ski about 9 miles to the trailhead.

The trailhead is located about a half mile east of Wonder Lake Campground, at an altitude of 2,100 feet. The trail goes almost due south through wooded, rolling terrain for 2 ¼ miles to the north bank of the McKinley River. Fording the McKinley River could be considered the most hazardous objective danger of the Muldrow Route. The route heads southeast across the river for 1 ¾ miles, and depending on the season (it is usually frozen until the end of April) and time of day (the river usually crests in late afternoon or early evening during the summer), the braided channels can be few, shallow, and simple to ford or float across or many, deep, and severe. At the far bank of the river, the approach to McGonagall Pass (the Traleika Spur and Muldrow Glacier routes) goes south, and the approach to the Muddy River (Wickersham Wall routes) goes west.

The route to McGonagall Pass heads south before turning slightly southwest, passing Turtle Hill on its southeast side. It then meanders between many small lakes and ponds before dropping down to the next

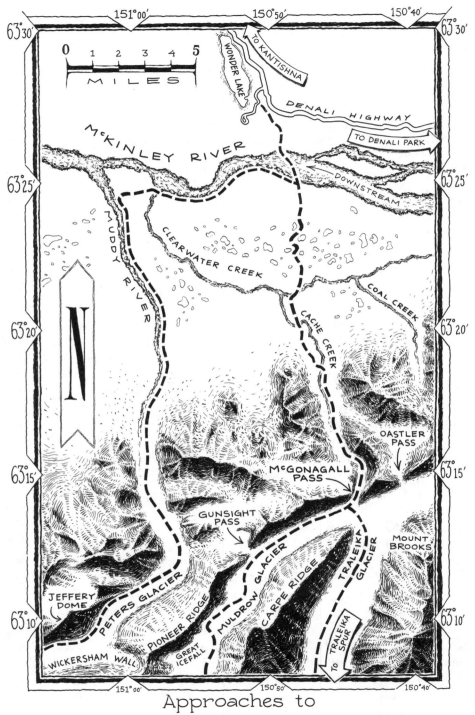

Approaches to
MᶜGONAGALL PASS
and
PETERS GLACIER

major stream crossing, Clearwater Creek, which is best done early in the morning. Clearwater Creek is about 10 miles from the Wonder Lake trailhead and 9 miles from McGonagall Pass. Go west along the south bank of Clearwater Creek for a half mile and then turn left (south) for a mile to Cache Creek, meeting it just downstream from a prominent moraine. After fording Cache Creek, the route goes southeast before turning south, climbing onto the crest of a poorly defined ridge that is west of Cache Creek. It gradually heads slightly southeast and crosses Cache Creek again, approximately 3 miles from the first crossing. The route heads east at first and then turns south, ascending the east bank of Cache Creek (crossing many side streams along the way) for 2¾ miles to the next crossing. The route ascends the west bank of the creek for a half mile before meeting the last significant crossing, immediately above a prominent fork in the stream. The left fork leads to Oastler Pass, and the right fork leads to McGonagall Pass. The route ascends the right fork and climbs up the canyon for 2½ miles to the summit of McGonagall Pass, at an altitude of 5,732 feet, 19 miles from the trailhead. The walk-in may take from two to eight days, depending on the load carried, snow cover, and level of the McKinley River.

The routes on Wickersham Wall were first approached and climbed by hiking 30 miles from Wonder Lake, up the Muddy River to Peters Glacier. Leave the approach to McGonagall Pass on the south side of the McKinley River. Follow the south bank of the McKinley River downstream for 5½ miles to Clearwater Creek. Go up Clearwater Creek, cross it as soon as possible, and then head west into the thick spruce forest to meet the east bank of the Muddy River, approximately 2 miles after leaving the McKinley River. Ascend the east bank of the Muddy River for about 7 miles to the end of the timber. Move to the right and follow the center of this barren valley, but remain to the left of the main channel of the Muddy River. Pass through (or over) two ancient moraines and then go slightly left and ascend the east side of Peters Glacier. Continue up the glacier to where it makes a sharp turn to the right (southwest) immediately beneath Wickersham Wall; the small valley to the left leads to Gunsight Pass and Muldrow Glacier. A minimum of three days of hiking is needed to reach this point, and another three to four days may be needed to continue up Peters Glacier to the base of one of the routes on Wickersham Wall. It may be prudent to climb high on one of the 5,000- to 6,000-thousand foot peaks to the east to scout out the next 5 miles of the jumbled maze of Peters Glacier.

Peters Glacier surged in 1986, and the current approach to Wickersham Wall now begins from Kahiltna Base, 17 miles away on the other (south) side of the mountain. Follow the Washburn Route up Kahiltna Glacier to Kahiltna Pass, which separates Kahiltna Glacier from Peters Basin. The north side of

Denali from the northeast. R. J. SECOR

Kahiltna Pass may be corniced, and crevasses, avalanches, and hanging seracs increase the difficulties and hazards. The pass has been directly descended to Peters Basin, and this is easy when the slope is stable. An alternative route heads west from the top of Kahiltna Pass and goes over (or very close to) the summit of 10,790-foot Mount Capps before descending its north rib. The approach then descends the northwest edge of Peters Basin, alternating between the moraine and the glacier itself to minimize encounters with crevasses. Continue down to the Tluna Icefall, reportedly the biggest icefall in the Alaska Range. The icefall is best passed on its northwest side, followed by a descent of Peters Glacier to the bottom of either the Harvard Route or the Canadian Route on Wickersham Wall. Another approach to Wickersham Wall is the Peters Basin Cutoff, described in chapter 3.

Further reading: *ANAM* (1982): 22–24; *ANAM* (1989): 29.

TRALEIKA SPUR—ALASKA GRADE 3

This 4-mile-long spur divides the main Traleika Glacier from its west fork. It could be considered the north fork of the East Buttress, but the route ends in the small basin at 13,900 feet beneath Thayer Basin without ever touching the crest of the buttress. It was first climbed May 25, 1972, by Pat Stewart,

Jock Jacober, Craig Schmidt, John G. Johnson, William Ruth, and David Pettigrew. This party of Alaskans took an astonishing fifty-two days to approach (one group from Denali Park, 95 miles away, and another from Kantishna, 40 miles away), climb the route, and hike out.

Head south from McGonagall Pass, cross Muldrow Glacier, and ascend Traleika Glacier for 8 miles to the base of the spur at 7,000 feet. The route starts by ascending the icefall on the northeastern side of the spur. A chute on the right side of the icefall was dubbed "Bertha" by the first ascent party because of its active avalanches. Climb the broken face to the left of Bertha, but to the right of the exposed rock face, to a campsite at 8,500 feet. The route continues up and left, ascending the steep face leading to the large plateau east of Point 12,060 feet. The first ascent party established its second camp on the southern edge of the plateau. Ascend the left side of the face to the small plateau at 11,000 feet, southeast of Point 12,060 feet, where there is a campsite. Climb the east ridge of Point 12,200+ feet, traverse the point, and descend to the col at 11,500 feet (another campsite). Traverse the north side of the ridge just below its crest, keeping underneath, and sometimes passing over cornices to Point 12,355 feet. Descend the southwest side of Point 12,355 feet to the basin between the two icefalls of the West Fork of Traleika Glacier. Pass the upper icefall on its left side and continue to Thayer Basin. The first ascent party summited the South Peak via Thayer Ridge (described in chapter 6 under South Buttress: Thayer Route) and descended the Traleika Spur.

Further reading: *AAJ* (1963): 453–60; *AAJ* (1973): 289–93.

BUTTE DIRECT—ALASKA GRADE 5

This difficult forty-pitch route ascends the rock wall near the head of the West Fork of Traleika Glacier, ending atop Karstens Ridge below Browne Tower. It was first climbed on May 9, 1997, by Jim Wilson and Jim Blow. Although the name of this route is "Direct," the first ascent party climbed it indirectly. They spent five days climbing twenty-five pitches of loose rock and rappelled from the top of the rock, skied down Traleika Glacier, climbed up Muldrow Glacier to Karstens Ridge, and descended from the top of the route back to their previous high point. They then climbed 1,200 feet of ice back to the top of the route. They continued up Harper Glacier to the summit (delayed by a ten-day storm) and then descended the Washburn Route for a total time of forty-three days.

Extreme caution is advised, as the West Fork of Traleika Glacier can be swept by huge avalanches, as can the route itself. After traversing the glacier, start by climbing a snow fan in the center of the rock face. Three

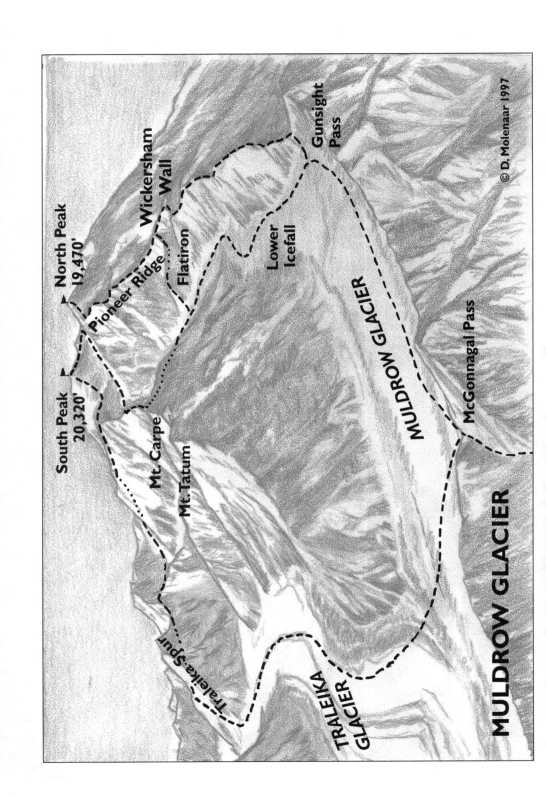

South Peak 20,320'

North Peak 19,470'

Wickersham Wall

Pioneer Ridge

Flatiron

Gunsight Pass

Lower Icefall

Mt. Carpe

Mt. Tatum

Traleika Spur

MULDROW GLACIER

McGonnagal Pass

TRALEIKA GLACIER

MULDROW GLACIER

© D. Molenaar 1997

pitches up the snow lead to the base of a gully. Go up and to the right for one pitch over mixed rock and ice to a belay stance, and continue up and to the right over YDS 5.5 rock to the base of a steep snowfield. One pitch up, the snow ends at the base of a large rock, where the first ascent party had its first campsite, despite its exposure to rockfall.

Continue up and to the right over mixed climbing for one pitch to the base of a horizontal snow slope. Go to the left and climb a gully to a snow slope, which is followed for two pitches to the base of a cliff, with a belay stance in a notch as protection from rockfall. Overcome the 180-foot cliff by means of YDS 5.8 climbing over loose rock and ice to the base of another snowfield. Two pitches up and to the right lead to the top of the snowfield, underneath an overhanging rock face. The first ascent party had its second campsite here, using the roof as protection from the severe rockfall.

Go down and to the right from the roof to a prominent inside corner with broken rock. Climb the corner, followed by a YDS 5.10 move over steep rock, and climb 75 feet to a belay stance. Another 75-foot inside corner leads to broken rock, overcome directly by means of YDS 5.9, A2 climbing. Ascend a small chimney and go into and out of a gully with some YDS 5.9 to 5.10 moves. Leave the gully on its right side to a ledge (a possible campsite) and then climb a left-facing dihedral. Leave the dihedral on its right side (YDS 5.10+) to another ledge (another campsite). Follow easy terrain to the right, then go up and to the left and climb a gully. When dry, this is YDS 5.5 to 5.6, but the first ascent party encountered waves of spindrift. Five pitches then lead up and to the right to a snow and ice field. Climb the steep snow and ice to a ridge that divides the upper part of the face. Traverse to the left under a broken rock face for several pitches before heading up into a gully system. This leads to an overhanging ice wall, overcome by eight to ten pitches of mixed climbing, YDS 5.5 to 5.8. The last pitch leads to the left under the overhanging icefall and ends on a snowfield. Go to the left and climb onto the large ridge that leads to Karstens Ridge, 1 mile distant.

MULDROW GLACIER—ALASKA GRADE 2

This route has also been called Karstens Ridge. It is the route used on the first ascent of Denali by Walter Harper, Harry P. Karstens, Robert G. Tatum, and Reverend Hudson Stuck, the Episcopal Archdeacon of the Yukon, on June 7, 1913, with support from Johnny and Esaias, two Native American teenagers. The route was pioneered, however, by the 1910 Sourdough Expedition, which succeeded in climbing the lower (but more difficult) North Summit of Denali, and by the 1912 Parker-Browne expedition, which almost reached the higher South Summit. This route description is of the Denali Pass variation ascended on July 6, 1947, by Bradford Washburn, Barbara Washburn, James Gale, William Hackett, Robert Lange, William Deeke, Bob Craig, and George Browne (the son of Belmore Browne). The Denali Pass variation is preferred, because it avoids the numerous crevasses on upper Harper Glacier, and it also allows climbers to see inclement weather approaching from the southwest.

Muldrow Glacier is heavily crevassed, and the route is exposed to avalanches. The main technical challenge is ascending Karstens Ridge, which gains 3,600 feet with small benches and steps with angles up to 45 degrees, but these difficulties are not as sustained as the headwall on the Washburn Route. After the almost 20-mile approach hike, the climbing route covers 18 miles one way, with more than 14,000 feet of gain to the South Summit. Expeditions have placed as many as eight camps along this route and typically take from eighteen to thirty-two days round-trip from Wonder Lake; a few parties traverse Denali, however, and descend the Washburn Route to Kahiltna Base.

Muldrow Glacier is less than 100 feet below the summit of McGonagall Pass. Muldrow is one of the more active glaciers on Denali, and it has a history of surges that, during some years, have made it impassable. The current route generally keeps to the right (northern) side of the glacier for about 5 miles, passing Gunsight Mountain and Gunsight Pass, to the Lower Icefall. (Hudson Stuck's party in 1913 and the 1931 Lindley-Liek Expedition kept to the left [south] side of the glacier and bypassed the Lower Icefall on its left [south] side, however.) Many parties pass through the Lower Icefall on its extreme right (northern) edge to minimize encounters with crevasses, but this route is exposed to avalanches from the hanging glacier that looms overhead along Pioneer Ridge. Other parties climb directly through the Lower Icefall, avoiding the hanging glacier but risking encounters with crevasses and seracs.

Above the Lower Icefall, the route moves left and ascends the middle portion of the glacier, passing the Hill of Cracks (a large crevassed area) on its left side. After 2 miles, it approaches the bottom of the Great Icefall at approximately 8,500 feet. At this point, the route goes left to the base of Mount Carpé and then goes to the right (southwest), ascending Muldrow Glacier along the base of Mount Koven for about 2 miles to the bottom of Karstens Ridge; this section of the route is exposed to avalanches from the hanging glaciers on the northwest sides of Mounts Carpé and Koven. An alternative but very intricate route passes the Great Icefall on its right side.

Karstens Notch or Karstens Col is marked on the USGS and the Washburn maps, but the couloir leading to the col is very steep. The next couloir to the right seems to be the best for attaining the crest of the ridge. Karstens Ridge is a knife-edge. Follow its crest upward to a prominent step at 12,100

Muldrow Glacier and Pioneer Ridge. Jim Okonek, K2 Aviation

feet, the only campsite along the entire ridge, which is, in reality, atop a huge cornice. The upper part of the ridge is known as The Coxcomb, and this is the crux of the Muldrow Glacier route. The angle varies between 30 and 45 degrees, and it is typically icy in the early season, but in late June and July,

Football Field. R. J. SECOR

new snow may make it necessary to shovel one's way upward. The ridge ends at the boulders of Parker Pass at the base of Browne Tower at 14,600 feet, an exposed but scenic campsite.

Parker Pass is not really a pass but a bench that is beneath the rock slabs of the South Peak's northeast ridge and Harper Icefall. This passage leads to Harper Glacier. The route goes to the north side of Harper Glacier and passes the lower icefall on its right (north) side at 16,000 feet. Continue up the glacier and pass the upper icefall at 17,000 feet, keeping to its right side. Ascend Harper Glacier to Denali Pass at 18,200 feet.

Denali Pass is an exposed, windy place, and most expeditions have their high camp at or just below the 18,000-foot level on the east side of the pass. Go left (south) from Denali Pass and ascend the east side of the poorly defined ridge. Some parties have gotten lost descending this slope (including the tragic 1967 Wilcox expedition, in which seven climbers lost their lives), and this section of the route must be well wanded. At least 100 wands, placed 100 feet apart, are needed to mark the route from Denali Pass to the summit, or 125 wands from 18,000 feet to the summit. There may be a weather sensor near 19,000 feet, located atop the Zebra Rocks northwest of Archdeacon's Tower, but this device has a history of blowing away. Pass Archdeacon's Tower on its right (west) side, and descend slightly to the Football Field, a surprisingly large, flat basin at 19,500 feet. The summit headwall rises ahead, and the best route is to ascend its right (west) side to Kahiltna Horn. Turn left, and taking care to avoid the cornices and steep slopes on the southern side, follow the ridge upward to the summit.

Further reading: *AAJ* (1933): 35–68; *AAJ* (1943): 1–13; *AAJ* (1948): 40–58; *ANAM* (1971): 16; *ANAM* (1977): 17; *ANAM* (1979): 19; *ANAM* (1981): 21–24; *ANAM* (1986): 20–21; *ANAM* (1993): 17–19; *ANAM* (1997): 12–13; Wayne P. Merry, "Disaster on Mount McKinley," *Summit*, December 1967, pp. 2–9; Kendall Williams, "McKinley Odyssey," *Climbing*, March–April 1974, pp. 16–20; Howard Snyder, *Hall of the Mountain King* (New York: Charles Scribner's Sons, 1973); Joe Wilcox, *White Winds* (Los Alamitos, CA: Hwong Publishing Company, 1981).

PARKER-BROWNE VARIATION—ALASKA GRADE 2

This was the route followed by Herschel Parker, Belmore Browne, and Merl LaVoy on June 29, 1912. This party did not summit. They had reached the top of Farthing Horn (20,125 feet), 1,000 horizontal feet and 200 vertical feet from the summit of the South Peak, when a violent storm stopped them. Belmore Browne continued on his hands and knees to a point only 660 horizontal feet and less than 150 vertical feet from the true summit. The first ascent of this route was completed May 6, 1932, by Harry J. Liek, Alfred D. Lindley, Erling Strom, and Grant Pearson.

This variation leaves the Muldrow Glacier route at approximately 16,500 feet on Harper Glacier, above the lower icefall. It traverses across the glacier and meets the northeast ridge of the South Summit at the col at 17,200 feet. Ascend the rocky crest of the ridge (or the snow slopes on the north) to the plateau at 18,700 feet. The plateau marks the base of a depression on the northeast side of the South Peak, with two vague ridges rising above it. Climb the right (northwest) ridge and continue over the top of Farthing Horn to the summit.

Further reading: *AAJ* (1933): 36–44; Belmore Browne, *The Conquest of Mt. McKinley* (Boston: Houghton Mifflin, 1956).

STUCK VARIATION—ALASKA GRADE 2

This is the route of the first ascent. It leaves the Muldrow Glacier route above the upper icefall of Harper Glacier at 17,500 feet. It goes south, climbs to the plateau at 18,700 feet, and then heads up and left to the little draw between Carter Horn and Farthing Horn. It then climbs the east slope of the South Peak, avoiding Farthing Horn.

Further reading: Hudson Stuck, *The Ascent of Denali* (Seattle: The Mountaineers, 1977).

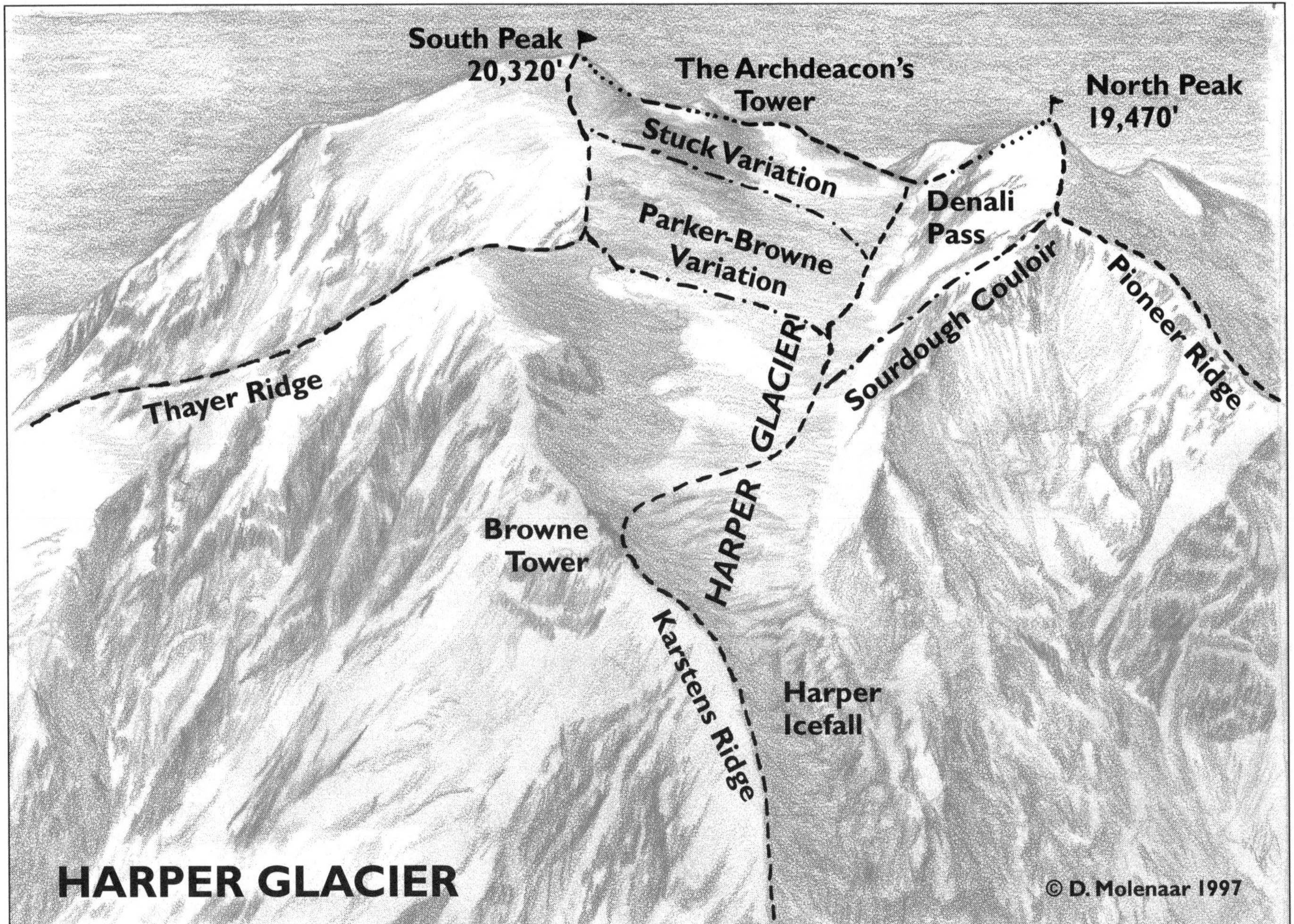

HARPER GLACIER

North Peak
19,470'

Pioneer Ridge

The Archdeacon's Tower

Denali Pass

Stuck Variation

Sourdough Couloir

Parker-Browne Variation

HARPER GLACIER

Harper Icefall

South Peak
20,320'

Karstens Ridge

Browne Tower

Thayer Ridge

© D. Molenaar 1997

Harper Glacier. JIM OKONEK, K2 AVIATION

SOURDOUGH COULOIR VARIATION—ALASKA GRADE 2

This is the route to the summit of the North Peak climbed by Billy Taylor and Pete Anderson on April 10, 1910. They made this ascent in one day from the 11,000-foot level of Muldrow Glacier. Another member of the party, Charley McGonagall, carried a 14-foot spruce pole as far as 18,800 feet before turning back. The pole could be seen by Hudson Stuck's party in 1913, who confirmed this remarkable climb.

The Sourdough Couloir starts from the 16,000-foot level of Harper Glacier on the right (north) side of the lower icefall. It rises 2,000 feet with angles up to 40 degrees and ends atop Pioneer Ridge. Go left and follow the ridge to the summit.

Further reading: *ANAM* (1977): 15–16.

ICE COULOIR VARIATION—ALASKA GRADE 2

This couloir leaves Harper Glacier at 17,300 feet, near the level of the upper icefall. It was first climbed on June 30, 1966, by Bruce Gilbert, Douglas Bingham, and Rudolf Schmid. This 1,500-foot, 55-degree couloir ends at the far eastern edge of the plateau that is southwest of the North Peak. The first ascent party continued directly up the south face of the North Peak, meeting the west ridge a short distance from the summit.

Further reading: *AAJ* (1967): 343.

NORTH PEAK FROM DENALI PASS VARIATION—ALASKA GRADE 2

This route was climbed on May 9, 1932, by Harry J. Liek, Alfred D. Lindley, Erling Strom, and Grant Pearson. Climb north from the basin that is immediately east of Denali Pass to the southeast face of Point 18,990 feet. Upon meeting the rocks, traverse up and right along a ledge system to the large plateau that is southwest of the North Peak. From the plateau, either climb to the summit of the North Peak directly or continue north and follow the west ridge to the summit.

Further reading: *AAJ* (1933): 36–44.

PIONEER RIDGE—ALASKA GRADE 3

Pioneer Ridge is the northeast ridge of the North Peak. This route was first climbed on July 23, 1961, by Sev Heiberg, Larry Fowler, Dietrich Haumann,

Donald Lyon, and Adolf Bauer. It covers about 5 miles and almost 10,000 feet of gain from Muldrow Glacier and involves steep climbing along this exposed (in terms of terrain and weather) ridge. The total time needed to ascend this route from Wonder Lake is twenty to thirty-five days.

Ascend Muldrow Glacier to the 10,000-foot level. Leave the Muldrow Glacier route here and find a way across the heavily crevassed glacier to the foot of the northeast ridge of the Flatiron. Ascend the sharp northeast ridge of the Flatiron and traverse the southern side of its crest to meet Pioneer Ridge at Point 12,545 feet, the first campsite. Climb the ridge above by keeping to its right (northwest) side, and near 13,500 feet, traverse to the right and climb a long snow chute that leads to the top of Taylor Spur at 15,070 feet, the second camp. The ridge goes up and down for half a mile beyond Taylor Spur without gaining any real altitude; there is a campsite near 16,000 feet. Above 16,000 feet, the route ascends rock along the crest of Pioneer Ridge for a short distance, and then there is a long traverse to the right (west), across many snow patches and gullies. This is followed by some scrambling up a minor rock rib and then a 200-foot, 50-degree snow chute that leads to the top of a spur that meets Pioneer Ridge from the northwest near 17,000 feet. The difficulties ease above 17,000 feet (the last campsite), and the route continues along the ridge (more or less) to the summit of the North Peak.

Further reading: *AAJ* (1962): 39–42; CAJ (1962): 75–88; ANAM (1981): 15.

PIONEER RIDGE: COMPLETE—ALASKA GRADE 3

This route ascends Pioneer Ridge starting from Gunsight Pass. It was first climbed on July 8, 1988, by Rowan Laver, Chuck Maffei, Jim Cancroft, and Randy Waitman. This 11-mile-long ridge gains almost 13,000 feet. The lower part of Pioneer Ridge is a sharp, exposed crest. The first ascent party found the 2-mile lower Sharp Ridge to be snow covered, with cornices and managed to traverse from 9,200 feet to 10,500 feet in one day over a period of fourteen hours, using running belays except on the most difficult pitches. (Although this part of the route went quickly, they spent a total of thirty-three days approaching and climbing this route from Wonder Lake, dealing with crevasses, weather, avalanches, cornices, and other Denali miseries.) The rest of the ridge to the Flatiron spur is broad, with less exposure. Continue to the summit of the North Peak over upper Pioneer Ridge.

Further reading: *AAJ* (1989): 84–89; *ANAM* (1977): 15–16.

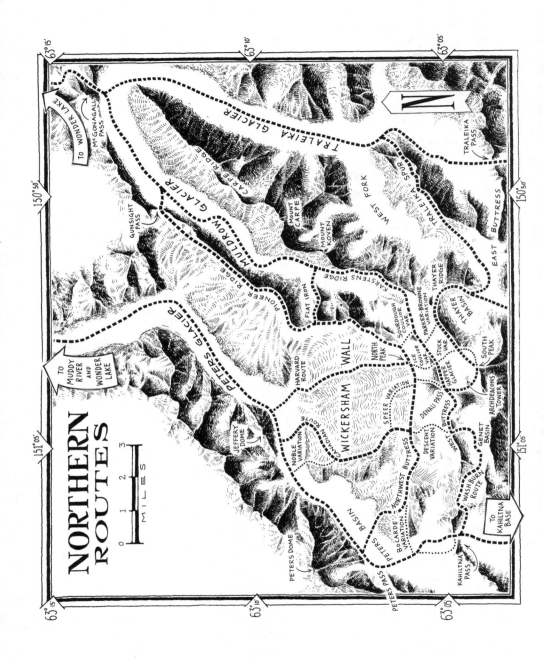

NORTHERN ROUTES

MILES
0 1 2 3

N

TO WONDER LAKE

McGONAGALL PASS

TRALEIKA GLACIER

CARPE RIDGE

GUNSIGHT PASS

MULDROW GLACIER

TRALEIKA PASS

WEST FORK

MOUNT CARPE

MOUNT KOVEN

TRALEIKA SPUR

EAST BUTTRESS

PIONEER RIDGE

KARSTENS RIDGE

FLAT IRON

THAYER RIDGE

THAYER BASIN

PETERS GLACIER

TO MUDDY RIVER AND WONDER LAKE

HARVARD ROUTE

WICKERSHAM WALL

NORTH PEAK

SOURDOUGH COULOIR VAR.

PARKER-BROWNE VARIATION

ICE COULOIR VAR.

STUCK VAR.

HARPER GLACIER

SOUTH PEAK

JEFFERY DOME

NOBLE VARIATION

CANADIAN ROUTE

SPEER VARIATION

DENALI PASS

WEST BUTTRESS

ARCHDEACONS TOWER

GENET BASIN

DESCENT VARIATION

PETERS DOME

NORTHWEST BUTTRESS

BOCARDE VARIATION

WASHBURN ROUTE

TO KAHILTNA BASE

PETERS BASIN

PETERS PASS

KAHILTNA PASS

WICKERSHAM WALL: HARVARD ROUTE—ALASKA GRADE 4

Wickersham Wall is leviathan. This 3-mile-wide face rises more than 14,000 feet in 4 miles. There are very few mountain faces in the world with such great vertical relief. The largest single vertical rise in the world is the 14,678-foot Rupal Face of Nanga Parbat, the ninth highest mountain in the world, located at the far western edge of the Himalaya in Pakistan.

This route was climbed on July 16, 1963, by members of the Harvard Mountaineering Club: Don Jensen, Dave Roberts, Peter Carman, John Graham, Richard Millikan, Hank Abrons, and Christopher Goetze. It makes a direct ascent to the summit of the North Peak from a rock spur between two icefalls that drop onto Peters Glacier. The objective dangers of this route are substantial, with serious exposure to rockfall and avalanches. As of this writing, it has never been repeated.

The Harvard Route starts from the 5,500-foot level of Peters Glacier, opposite Jeffery Dome. Begin by climbing the icefall to the right of the spur, and climb onto its crest at approximately 6,650 feet, the first campsite. Ascend the spur for eight pitches of mixed rock and snow climbing (to YDS 5.5); this section of the route ends at a shelf above a verglas-covered slab. The spur above the shelf is less steep, consisting of a corniced, soft snow crest, four rock gendarmes (the most difficult rock gendarme, the fourth, was overcome by means of a point of aid), and finally Shady Lane, a 70-degree ice headwall. At this point (8,500 feet), the spur merges into a 500-foot snow bulge, the last pitch of which is near-vertical ice. The next obstacle is a 100-foot overhanging ice cliff at 10,300 feet; the first ascent party found this broken by a narrow 60-degree chimney, dubbed "The Icebox." The route above The Icebox continues up the shallow snow spur, marked by broad slopes, cliffs, crevasses, and gullies, to 14,500 feet, level with the huge snowfield on the north face of the North Peak. Traverse up and right until directly beneath the summit of the North Peak. Continue straight up the north face to the top of the North Peak.

Further reading: *AAJ* (1964): 47–51; *Harvard Mountaineering* 17 (May 1965): 27–36; Gary Speer, "North Face Summer," *Summit* (January-February 1983): 16–18.

WICKERSHAM WALL: CANADIAN ROUTE—ALASKA GRADE 2

This route ascends the western rib of Wickersham Wall. It was first climbed on June 13, 1963, by Hans Gmoser, Gunther Prinz, and Hans Schwarz; other members of the expedition were Canadians Patrick Boswell, Leopold Grillmair, and Dietrich Raubach and Americans Henry Kauffman and Tom

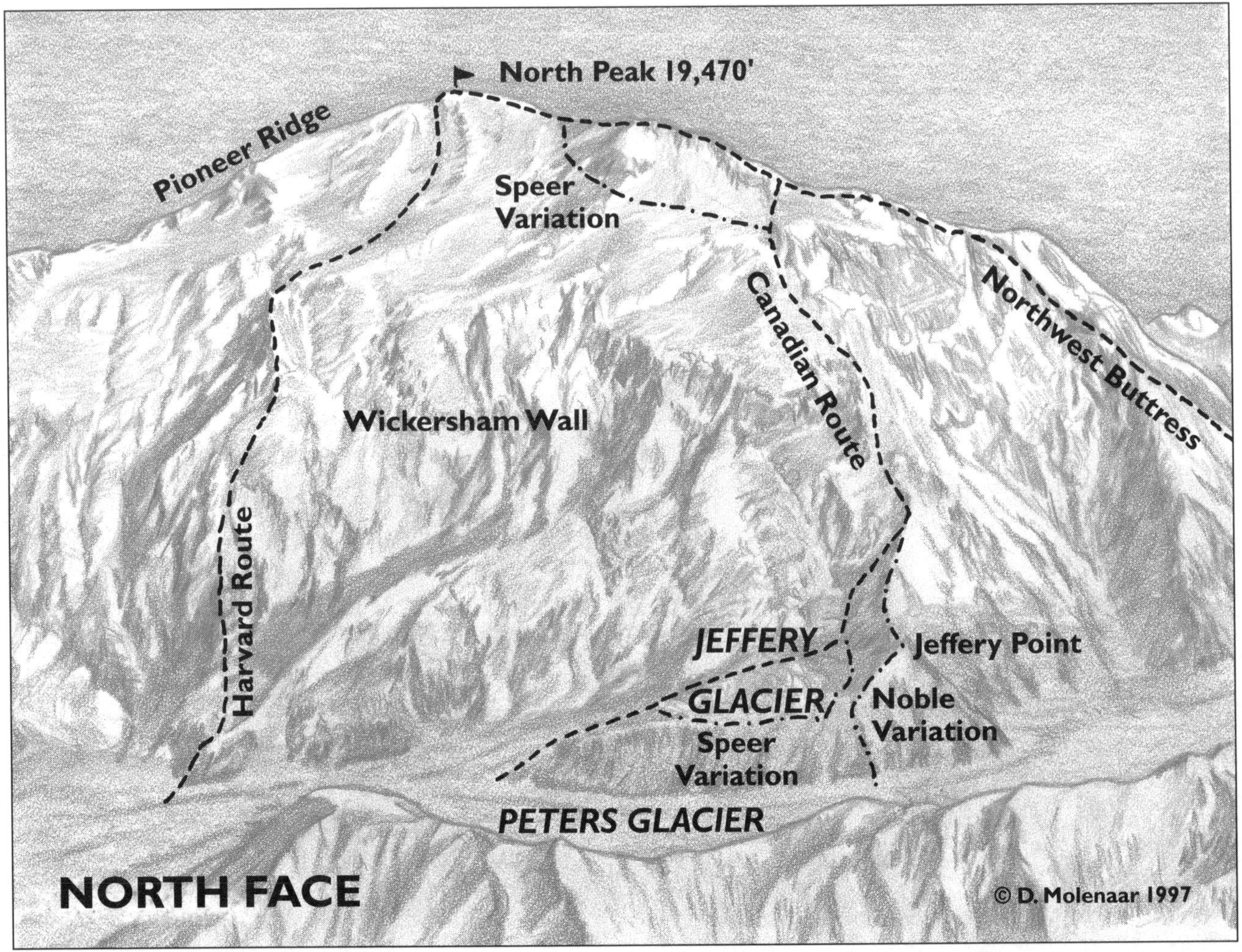

© D. Molenaar 1997

Northwest Buttress

Jeffery Point

Noble
Variation

Canadian Route

JEFFERY

GLACIER

Speer
Variation

▲ North Peak 19,470'

Speer
Variation

PETERS GLACIER

Wickersham Wall

Pioneer Ridge

Harvard Route

NORTH FACE

North Face. Austin Post, No. F645-95, USGS Ice and Climate Project, Geodata Center, University of Alaska

Spencer. This route is technically easy, but it is exposed to avalanches. It gains almost 13,500 feet over a distance of 7 miles after the approach is completed. Parties have established from four to six camps, and fourteen to thirty days' total time is needed for this route.

Leave Peters Glacier at the 5,700-foot level and ascend Jeffery Glacier, passing the middle icefall on its left (south) side. One is exposed to hanging glaciers and seracs crossing Jeffery Glacier, and the danger from avalanches is severe. Continue up the upper icefall and climb onto the crest of the ridge (snow and ice slopes up to 45 degrees) at the 9,000-foot level south of Jeffery Point. The ridge passes over crevasses and short steps of 45 to 60 degrees, to 11,000 feet; this was Judge James Wickersham's high point, reached on June 20, 1903. The ridge becomes less definite at this point, and the next 1,500 feet of the route are the most exposed to avalanches. The ridge (exposed, but at an angle of perhaps 50 degrees) returns briefly above this slope at 12,800 feet, and this leads to the upper part of Wickersham Wall. The route continues up the extreme left edge of a rock band and meets the Northwest Buttress at 16,600 feet. The rest of the route continues up the crest of the Northwest Buttress (described in chapter 3) to the summit of the North Peak.

Further reading: *AAJ* (1947): 283–93; *AAJ* (1962): 49–50; *AAJ* (1964): 43–46; *ANAM* (1984): 15–16; *Couloir* 7, no. 1 (October-November 1994): 16–25.

NOBLE VARIATION—ALASKA GRADE 2
This variation was climbed on May 18, 1983, by Chris Noble and Kelly McKean; other members of this expedition were Rick Wyatt and Evelyn Lees. They made a direct ascent up the icefall that drops directly onto Peters Glacier, almost due north of Jeffery Point. They then climbed onto the crest of the ridge, traversed Jeffery Point, and continued up the ridge, encountering a 60-degree ice cliff at the 8,500-foot level.

Further reading: *AAJ* (1984): 150–52.

SPEER VARIATION—ALASKA GRADE 2
This variation was climbed on June 15, 1983, by Gary Speer, Markus Hutnak, and Tim Gage. It leaves the Canadian Route at approximately 15,000 feet and traverses left, across the north face of the North Peak, and then ascends to the crest of the Northwest Buttress, meeting it at the first saddle west of the North Peak.

Further reading: *AAJ* (1984): 152–53; Gary Speer, "The Wickersham Wall," *Climbing* (November 1983): 28–32.

· CHAPTER 3 ·

Western Routes

These routes are approached from Kahiltna Base, the landing strip on the Southeast Fork of the Kahiltna Glacier, located at 7,200 feet, at the Denali Wilderness boundary. This is the most popular side of Denali, and there is usually a well-beaten path leading up the main Kahiltna Glacier by June of each year. Many assume that this side of Denali has been "climbed out," but there is great potential for new routes on Father and Son's Wall and the northwest face of West Buttress.

Most of these routes are approached via the Washburn Route. Exceptions include the Northwest Buttress, Father and Son's Wall and the northwest face of West Buttress, which are approached from Peters Basin. The crossing of Kahiltna Pass and its alternate, Mount Capps, is described in chapter 2. Another approach that has been used for Father and Son's Wall and northwest face of West Buttress is the Peters Basin Cutoff: Leave the Washburn Route at approximately 12,000 feet, near the bottom of Squirrel Hill. Descend the north side of the West Buttress toward the easternmost rock outcrop below the Washburn Route. Traverse along the bottom of these outcrops and cliffs to their lowest point, then descend, angling slightly left for approximately 500 feet until a small (30- to 40-foot) ice cliff becomes visible to the left (looking down). Traverse into the gully beneath this ice cliff and down-climb (or rappel) about 800 feet of sustained 45-degree ice; this is not for the faint of heart. This gully eventually widens into a snow or ice slope. Descend this slope, angling left, toward the bergschrund. Traverse to the left (looking down) for 200 to 300 feet, where it may be possible to climb down over the 'schrund. Continue descending the slope to the eastern lobe of Peters Basin.

WESTERN ROUTES

Denali from Kahiltna Base. R. J. Secor

NORTHWEST BUTTRESS—ALASKA GRADE 4

This route ascends the west buttress of the North Peak. After the approach, it covers 9 miles with approximately 12,000 feet of gain to the summit of the North Peak. Six camps have been placed on this route, and it may take from fifteen to thirty-one days round-trip. It was first climbed by Fred Beckey, Bill Hackett, Donald McLean, Henry Meybohm, and Charles R. Wilson on May 27, 1954. This party approached the mountain by flying from Lake Minchumina to a frozen lake at the base of Straightaway Glacier and hiking approximately 20 miles up the glacier and crossing Peters Pass before descending to the base of the route on Peters Glacier. The current approach is from Kahiltna Pass and/or Mount Capps, as described in chapter 2, or via the Peters Basin Cutoff, described earlier in this chapter. Descend to the 7,500-foot level of Peters Basin and move to the right (east) to the northern side of "Cook's Shoulder," the 10,500-foot outer edge of the Northwest Buttress. This was named after Dr. Frederick A. Cook, who attempted to climb Denali via this ridge during his 1903 expedition. Start by climbing a snow couloir, and then move to the right across a small triangular plateau at the 9,000-foot level. The route then zigzags up to the western ridge of Cook's

Shoulder. Continue up the ridge, which becomes a corniced coxcomb above 10,500 feet. The first ascent party established its first camp just beyond this coxcomb on the northern (left-hand) side of the ridge, about 300 feet below the crest, for protection from high winds.

Beyond the coxcomb is the first of three rock obstacles encountered along the Northwest Buttress. The first ascent party dubbed this "Abruzzi Ridge," probably reflecting Bill Hackett's aspirations on K2 (he later led an attempt on Abruzzi Ridge on K2 in 1960). Climb the right (south) side of Abruzzi Ridge for approximately 1,000 feet to the right-hand side of Pyramid I. This cliff consists of snow and ice over poor reddish brown slate, with the steepest (but fun) climbing near the top of the pyramid, at an elevation of 12,500 feet. The route continues up the crest to the base of the next impediment, Pyramid II, at 13,100 feet. Bypass this by traversing to the left (north), across a large, sloping cirque (the first ascent party's second camp) to a broad snow couloir (avalanche danger!) that leads back up to the crest of the Northwest Buttress at an elevation of 14,200 feet, well beyond the top of Pyramid II. Continue up the crest of the ridge to 14,800 feet, where the first ascent party placed its third camp, at the base of the last major rock problem.

In contrast to the rotten rock encountered on the lower Northwest Buttress, this rock consists of large blocks of frost-shattered pink and orange granite. The climbing is low YDS class 5 over its lower portion, and the upper part is made up of steps every 30 to 40 feet that end at a good campsite at 15,600 feet. Continue ascending the ridge that leads northeast to Point 16,620 feet, and continue up more steep snow and ice along the crest of the Northwest Buttress to the plateau that is southwest of the summit of the North Peak. Climb to the beautiful summit of the North Peak via its west ridge.

The first ascent party descended the Northwest Buttress. The North Peak can be traversed by descending to Denali Pass; the ledge system that leads down across the southeast face of Point 18,990 is not readily apparent from above, but it can be found. Another option is to descend the Northwest Buttress route to the 16,600-foot level. Head south to Uemura Basin, south of the Northwest Buttress and north of the West Buttress of the South Peak. From there, it is relatively easy to meet the Washburn Route along the West Buttress. One can either continue down the Washburn Route to Kahiltna Base or ascend the upper part of the Washburn Route to the top of the South Peak, the true summit of Denali.

Further reading: *AAJ* (1955): 70–77.

BOCARDE VARIATION—ALASKA GRADE 4

This could be considered the modern variation to the Northwest Buttress. The 1954 party wore rubber bunny boots and shoepacs with hinged crampons, as opposed to the stiff mountaineering boots and rigid crampons that are in common use today. It was first climbed on May 14, 1982, by John Rehmer and Jim Snyder, members of Gary Bocarde's Mountain Trip Expedition, which included David Shrimpton, John Stolpman, and Alan Novey. This party reached the top of Cook's Shoulder by climbing a 2,000-foot, 30- to 35-degree couloir on the west side of the shoulder. They then passed Abruzzi Ridge on its left side by climbing mixed rock and ice for two pitches. The crux of this variation (and the route) is Pyramid II, climbed directly via its west face, with very difficult climbing over steep ice and rotten rock. This could take a whole day of climbing to overcome, but it avoids the potentially dangerous snow couloir behind Pyramid II, and depending on conditions, it may be the only safe option. Finally, the last major rock problem can be bypassed by traversing up and left (on the north side of the buttress), past the rock to a snow couloir that leads up to the higher part of the Northwest Buttress.

Further reading: *AAJ* (1984): 148–50; *ANAM* (1983): 23–24.

FIRST BORN—ALASKA GRADE 4

This route climbs Father and Son's Wall, the 6,000-foot face between the eastern lobe of Peters Basin and the crest of the Northwest Buttress. The wall is only in condition when it is covered with frozen snow; otherwise, there is a lot of loose rock. First Born was first climbed July 2, 1995, by Steve House and Eli Helmuth. They approached the base of the route via the Peters Basin Cutoff from the 12,000-foot level of the Washburn Route. First Born starts by climbing the right side of a prominent snow gully on the left side of the bottom of Father and Son's Wall. Ascend this gully for approximately 400 feet, and then follow a narrow finger of ice that goes slightly right for 100 feet to a snowfield. Make a diagonal traverse up and right across the snowfield to the chimney in the first rock band. The first pitch in the right-trending, deep chimney is YDS 5.8, over bad rock with thin 70-degree ice; the second pitch features 60-degree ice.

A 45-degree snowfield leads to the second rock band, cut by a narrow, steep chimney. The first pitch in the chimney starts with 30 feet of vertical climbing. The second pitch is also steep, but the third pitch is moderate and ends with steep slab climbing; thin ice overlaying this 45-degree slope leads to the third rock band. The first ascent party climbed an 80-foot thin icicle

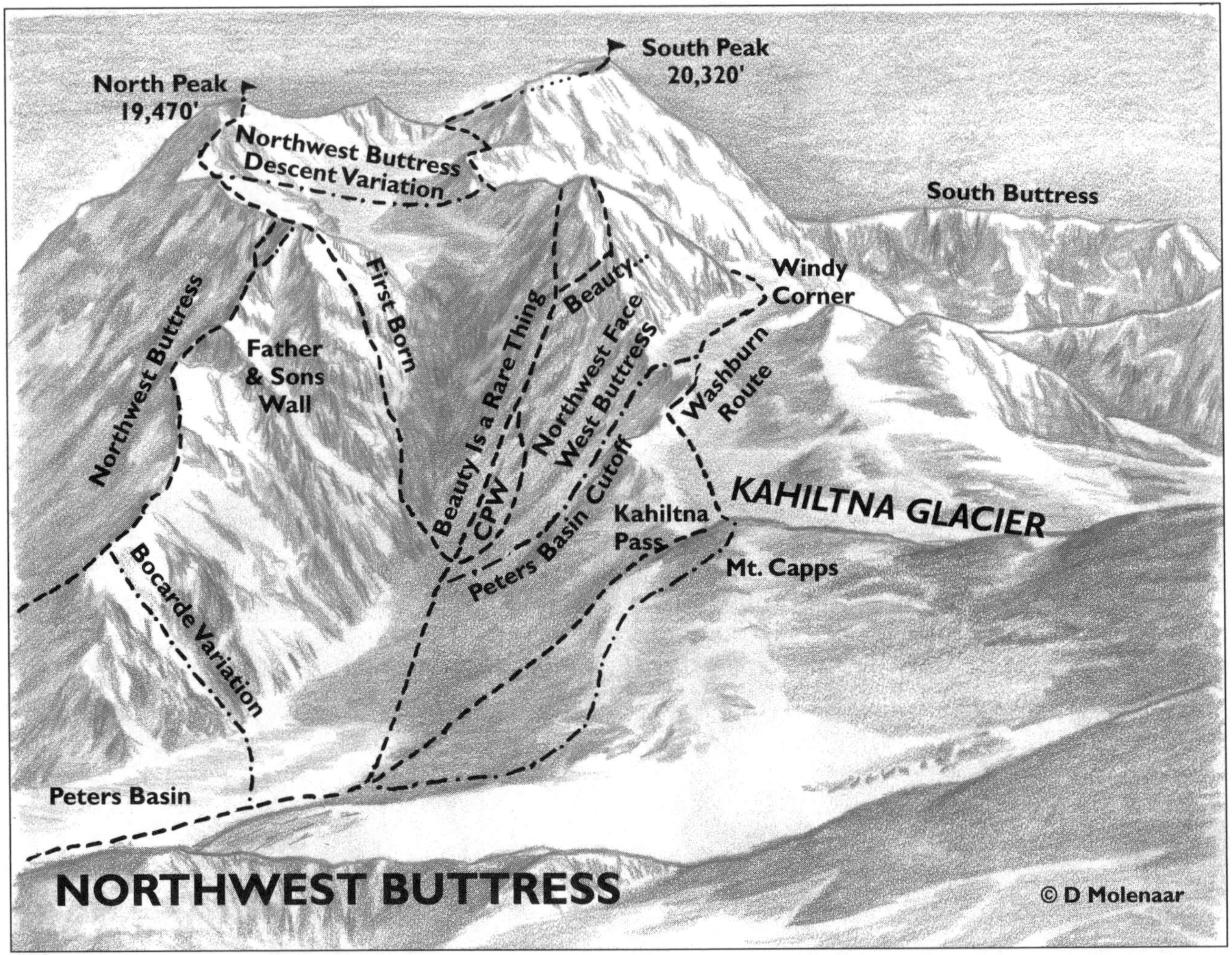

South Buttress

KAHILTNA GLACIER

© D Molenaar

South Peak
20,320'

Windy
Corner

Washburn
Route

Mt. Capps

Kahiltna
Pass

Peters Basin Cutoff

West Buttress

Northwest Face

Beauty

CPW

Beauty Is a Rare Thing

North Peak
19,470'

Northwest Buttress
Descent Variation

First Born

Father
& Sons
Wall

Northwest Buttress

Bocarde Variation

Peters Basin

NORTHWEST BUTTRESS

that drops from a slight, left-facing corner on the left side of the third rock band. (It is wise to view the third rock band from the base of the route before attempting an ascent, to ensure that the ice offers a way over this obstacle; it may be possible to bypass the third rock band on its far left side.) The rest of the route climbs ice fields of 40 to 55 degrees to the top of Father and Son's Wall (the crest of the Northwest Buttress) at 15,400 feet.

Further reading: *AAJ* (1996): 88–94.

BEAUTY IS A RARE THING—ALASKA GRADE 5

This route ascends the northwest face of the West Buttress, rising above the far eastern lobe of Peters Basin. Whereas Father and Son's Wall is condition-dependent, this face is almost always in shape. The steep terrain sheds excess snow, and the rock is more solid than that found on Father and Son's Wall. Beauty Is a Rare Thing was first climbed solo by Steve House on June 23, 1996, in 14½ hours round-trip from the 14,200-foot camp on the Washburn Route, approached via the Peters Basin Cutoff. It has more than 7,000 feet of gain over 1¼ climbing miles to the 16,000-foot crest of the West Buttress, not counting the approach. There aren't many bivouac sites, so it will probably appeal only to extreme climbers capable of making a one-day ascent. It starts by ascending the prominent narrow face (or broad couloir) in the middle of the northwest face of West Buttress. Approximately 1,800 feet of moderate ice leads to the major rock band on the face. The white spot on the rock band is, in reality, snow blasted onto the rock by spindrift. Move 150 feet to the right of the white spot to some water ice runnels. These start out at 15 feet wide and narrow to 2 feet after about 100 feet of climbing. Climb this series of vertical runnels for 200 to 300 feet to a small alcove. Two more runnels continue above the alcove. Climb the left one; it is very steep for the first 30 feet and then eases to 65 degrees and 1 foot wide. From the top of this runnel, traverse to the left for 60 feet over rock (YDS 5.8) to the bottom of a snow couloir. This couloir leans to the left for about 200 feet, averages 50 degrees, and has three chockstones that offer short, steep cruxes; bypass the last chockstone on its left side for 50 feet of excellent YDS 5.6 rock climbing. This couloir leads to the main ice gully system in the center of the upper part of northwest face of West Buttress. The route goes diagonally right up these gullies (40 to 50 degrees and 50 to 100 feet wide) to approximately 15,000 feet, where they fade into lower-angled rock. Go to the right and ascend a shallow ice rib to the prominent snowfield high on the west face of the West Buttress.

Further reading: *AAJ* (1997): 44–48.

COLLINS-POWERS-WALTER ROUTE—ALASKA GRADE 5

This route also ascends the northwest face of the West Buttress, rising above the far eastern lobe of Peters Basin. It was first climbed July 1, 1991, by Greg Collins, Philip Powers, and Tom Walter. Approach Peters Basin via Kahiltna Pass and Mount Capps, as described in chapter 2, or the Peters Basin Cutoff. The climbing starts by crossing the bergschrund and ascends the face to the right of Beauty Is a Rare Thing, consisting of about 2,000 feet of 55-degree snow, ice, and mixed climbing. It then goes up and left to a rock band, overcome by 200 feet of YDS class 5 rock climbing, followed by more mixed climbing that leads to the main ice gully system in the center of the upper part of the face. Beauty Is a Rare Thing goes up and right in this area, and the Collins-Powers-Walter (CPW) Route goes directly up and ascends the snowfield below Point 16,030 feet, the western summit of the West Buttress. Traverse the crest of the West Buttress to the top of the fixed ropes of the Washburn Route at 16,000 feet.

Further reading: *AAJ* (1992): 68–70.

A route to the right of the Collins-Powers-Walter Route was climbed in 1993 by Stephen Koch and Jeff Applebee. They traversed up and right, mostly over 55-degree ice, to the crest of the lower West Buttress below Windy Corner, and continued on to the 14,200-foot camp on the Washburn Route.

Further reading: *AAJ* (1994): 114.

DIRECT WEST BUTTRESS

The next six routes ascend the west and southwest faces of the middle portion of Denali's great West Buttress of the South Peak. This face rises 3,000 to 4,000 feet above the Washburn Route below Windy Corner. These routes are collectively referred to as the Direct West Buttress.

UPPER PETERS BASIN COULOIR—ALASKA GRADE 3

This route was ascended in May 1983 by Doug Van Etten and Marty Schmidt. It leaves the Washburn Route at approximately 12,000 feet and crosses the crest of the lower West Buttress, far above Peters Basin below. It traverses up and left to the prominent 45-degree couloir along the western edge of the buttress. The route then goes along the right edge of the big snowfield below Point 16,030 feet, the western summit of the West Buttress.

THUNDER RIDGE—ALASKA GRADE 3

This technical route involves thirty-four pitches of interesting but never diffi-cult climbing, mostly over snow and ice, with minimum exposure to objec-tive dangers. It was first climbed on June 29, 1982, by Michael Covington, Bill Holton, and Stan Olsen over a period of three days. The route starts at 12,700 feet and ascends a 50- to 60-degree narrow ice gully on the right side of the west ridge on the West Buttress itself. Six pitches in the gully lead to a prominent snow and ice ramp. The first ascent party camped here at an alti-tude of 13,300 feet. Four pitches up the ramp lead to "Windy Col," a small, narrow saddle that separates the ramp from a large couloir on the right. Go left and climb over snow with some rock for approximately 300 feet to the base of a snowfield that can be seen from the base of the route. Ascend the snowfield for about 200 feet, and then go to the right and follow the ridge for 300 feet to the "Niche," a perfect site for a three-person tent, between two rocks at an altitude of 14,400 feet. Just above the Niche, the ridge meets the large couloir to the right. Traverse up and right across the couloir to the large rock band looming above. Follow the base of the rock band up and right over 50-degree ice for four pitches to round a corner. This leads to a large couloir, which is ascended for 400 feet to the ridge atop the West Buttress. A knife-edged ridge then leads for four pitches to Point 16,030 feet.

Further reading: *AAJ* (1983): 144–46.

DIRECT WEST BUTTRESS—ALASKA GRADE 3

This route, the first to ascend the Direct West Buttress, parallels the Thunder Ridge Route. It was first climbed in June 1980 by Duane Muetzel, Ken Groff, Neal Beidleman, and Granger Banks. The first ascent party climbed from 12,700 feet to 16,100 feet in one sixteen-hour push. The route starts to the right of Thunder Ridge and traverses up and left across rock and snow to the crest of the ridge. It then meanders up 35- to 50-degree couloirs and rock ribs for 3,000 feet to the top of the buttress. The route continues along the crest of the upper West Buttress to meet the Washburn Route at the top of the fixed ropes.

Further reading: *AAJ* (1981): 152–53.

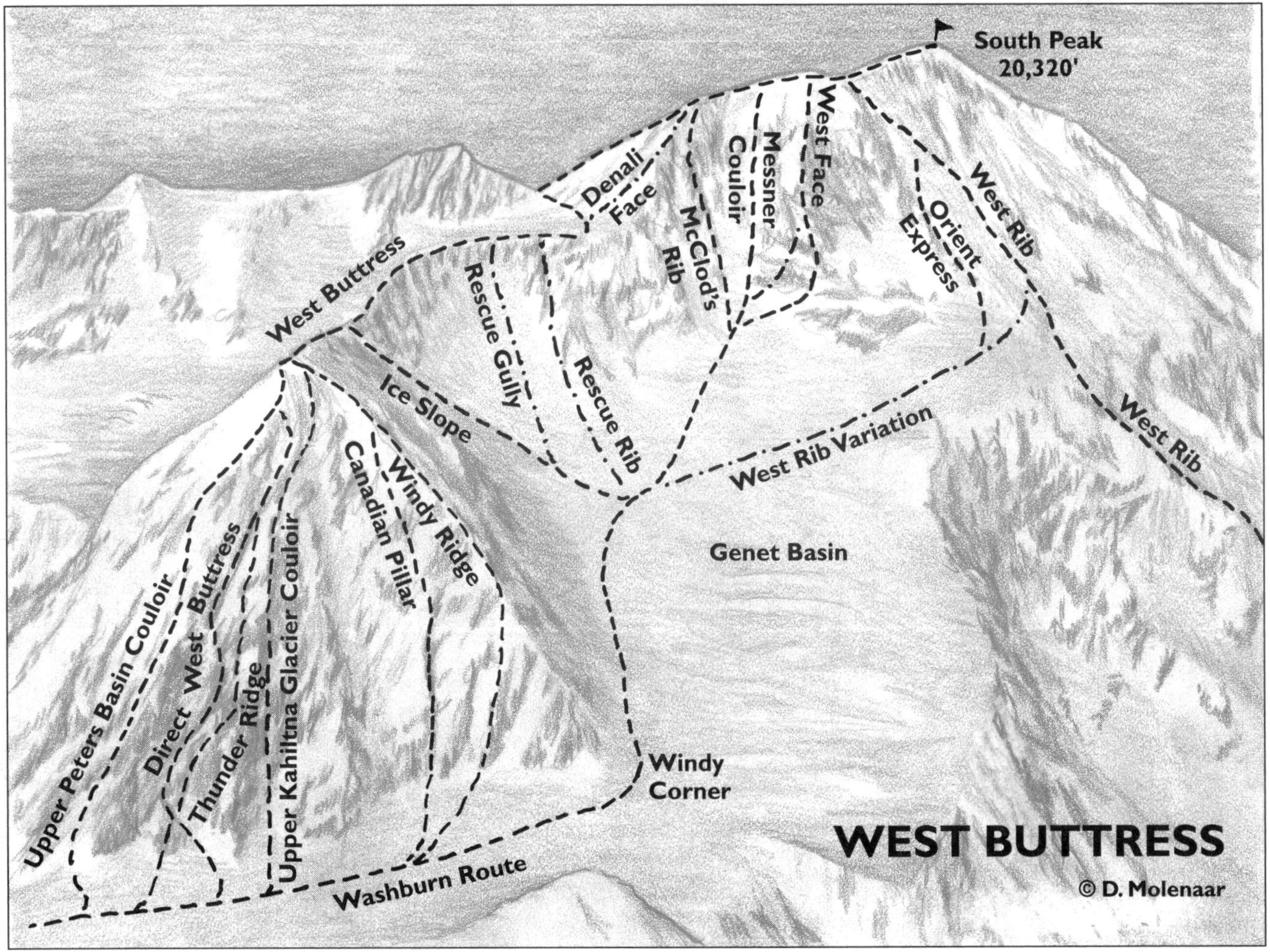

WEST BUTTRESS

© D. Molenaar

South Peak
20,320'

West Rib

West Rib

Orient
Express

West Face

Messner
Couloir

McClod's
Rib

West Rib Variation

Genet Basin

Denali
Face

Rescue Rib

Windy
Corner

Rescue Gully

Ice Slope

Windy Ridge

Canadian Pillar

Washburn Route

West Buttress

Upper Kahiltna Glacier Couloir

Thunder Ridge

Direct West Buttress

Upper Peters Basin Couloir

UPPER KAHILTNA GLACIER COULOIR—ALASKA GRADE 3

This route was first climbed May 29, 1990, by Canadians Timo Saukko and Peter Mattson, shortly after the first *ascent* of Trans Canada. The route ascends the first couloir to the right of Thunder Ridge. Take the right branch of the upper couloir to the top of the western summit of the West Buttress. The complete route consists of twenty-five pitches of very hard ice.

Further reading: *AAJ* (1991): 154–55; *CAJ* (1991): 87–88.

CANADIAN PILLAR—ALASKA GRADE 4

This route was first ascended on May 29, 1990, by Ross Cloutier, Mike Kurth, and Mario Bilodeau; this party had just completed the first ascent of Trans Canada with Saukko and Mattson. The route climbs the prominent rock pillar to the right of center on the southwest face of the Direct West Buttress. Eleven pitches of YDS 5.8 rock on the pillar itself lead to mixed snow and ice climbing. Continue slightly left and up the southwest face to meet the crest of Windy Ridge. Follow the ridge up to Point 16,030 feet.

Further reading: *AAJ* (1991): 154–55; *CAJ* (1991): 87–88.

WINDY RIDGE—ALASKA GRADE 3

This route was first climbed on May 27–28, 1982, by Bruce Hickok and Sabine Von Glinski. It starts by ascending the narrow, 800-foot, 60-degree couloir on the right side of the southwest face. The couloir ends atop the crest of the south ridge of the West Buttress. Ascend the YDS class 4 boulders along the ridge to Point 16,030 feet, and continue along the crest of the ridge to meet the Washburn Route at the top of the fixed ropes.

WASHBURN ROUTE—ALASKA GRADE 2

This route, the most popular, is commonly referred to as the West Buttress. It has been renamed here not only to honor Henry Bradford Washburn, Jr., but also to help prevent confusion of this route with the actual, physical West Buttress of the South Peak of Denali, which itself has a number of routes.

This route was discovered by Washburn. He described it in the 1947 *American Alpine Journal* as a possible new route to the summit. In 1949, he scouted this route from the air for the Office of Naval Research, seeking a shorter and easier route to Denali Pass for cosmic ray research. In 1951, he teamed up with William Hackett and James Gale, and the three of them summited on July 10. This party was flown onto Kahiltna Glacier by Terris Moore, who, at the time, was president of the University of Alaska. The other members of the expedition, Henry Buchtel, Barry Bishop, John Ambler, Jerry More, and T. Melvin Griffiths, summited on July 13 and 14, after approaching the mountain from Wonder Lake via Peters Pass and Kahiltna Pass. The first winter ascent was done by Art Davidson, Ray Genet, and Dave Johnston on March 1, 1967.

It involves 15.5 miles and about 13,500 feet of gain. The total time required to summit and return is fourteen to thirty days. Approximately 80 percent of all the climbers on Denali are on the Washburn Route, and it is not uncommon to have more than three hundred climbers on this route at one time. It is a recurring misperception among climbers, especially those who have never been on the route, that it is a crowded, dirty, littered slog to the apex of North America. But the majority of the thousands of mountaineers who have followed this route have done a remarkable job keeping it clean. And although the route is a slog up to 15,000 feet, above Genet Basin, it becomes aesthetic. The head wall between 15,000 and 16,000 feet is challenging, ascending the exposed crest of the upper West Buttress is like being

Kahiltna Base. R. J. SECOR

Climbing Kahiltna Glacier. R. J. SECOR

Camp at 7,800 feet, Kahiltna Glacier. R. J. SECOR

Below Kahiltna Glacier. R. J. SECOR

on the summit all day, and the route from 17,000 feet to the summit is intricate. The Washburn Route is a classic.

Many expeditions assume that there is safety in numbers and replace self-sufficiency with the deadly misperception that the crowds and the National Park Service ranger patrols will come to their aid in the event of trouble. All expeditions must make the commitment to be self-sufficient, and all mountaineers must climb smart.

Denali with the Northeast Fork, Kahiltna Glacier. R. J. Secor

Camp at 10,000 feet, Kahiltna Glacier. R. J. Secor

Climbing the Washburn Route. R. J. Secor

The Washburn Route begins at the 7,200-foot level of the Southeast Fork of Kahiltna Glacier at Kahiltna Base. The Talkeetna air taxis maintain a base camp here with a radio operator, and Denali National Park and Preserve rangers may be posted. The route goes west and descends "Heartbreak Hill" (which means that returning climbers have to *climb* 500 feet to reach Kahiltna Base) to meet the main branch of Kahiltna Glacier at the 6,700-foot level. Turn right (north) and ascend Kahiltna Glacier. Don't skirt the base of Mount Frances (peak, 10,450 feet), where there is danger from crevasses and avalanches; instead, ascend the middle of the glacier to the first slope or "hill" at the 7,000-foot level. I like to call this "Sled Hill," because it is at this point that climbers find out if their sled traces are adjusted properly for uphill travel. Sled Hill is marked by a series of large crevasses, and these are best bypassed to the left (west). The route stays in the middle of Kahiltna Glacier and heads northeast before turning north to reach the base of Ski Hill at the 7,800-foot level. This is the usual first campsite and is commonly referred to as the "8,000-foot camp." It is approximately 5 miles and takes heavily loaded climbers four to five hours from Kahiltna Base.

Ski Hill is marked by a long stretch of longitudinal crevasses (that is, they run up and down the glacier rather than across it). These are passed on their right (east) sides. If Ski Hill were located at a ski resort, it would have a green dot rating: It gains only 1,000 feet in a little more than a mile. The next

Approaching 11,000 feet, Washburn Route. R. J. Secor

Camp at 11,000 feet, Washburn Route. R. J. Secor

2 miles and 1,000 feet of gain lead to the 9,700-foot campsite (commonly referred to as the "10,000-foot camp") at the base of Kahiltna Pass, and this takes four to six hours from the 8,000-foot camp. This campsite is exposed to strong winds funneling through Kahiltna Pass, however, and some expeditions continue another two to three hours up the Washburn Route, which turns right (east) and climbs another mile to a small, shallow cul-de-sac at 11,000 feet. Although this latter campsite is protected from strong winds, it is potentially exposed to falling seracs and avalanches, and it seems to collect an inordinate amount of snow during storms. Most expeditions cache their skis or snowshoes here, and it is worth bringing a long pole to mark the cache site.

The slope behind (northeast from) the 11,000-foot camp is Motorcycle Hill. It climbs 400 feet to the crest of the lower West Buttress. The Washburn Route crosses the crest of the buttress, turns right (east), and traverses across the north slope, passing through a bowl. It then turns right and climbs Squirrel Hill to 12,200 feet, where the route meets a large bench located beneath the great cliffs of the middle portion of the West Buttress. The Washburn Route between 12,200 and 14,000 feet is exposed to avalanches, rockfall, and high winds, and camping cannot be recommended anywhere along this section. It is a long way from 11,000 feet to Genet Basin, however, and the best campsite here is at 12,900 feet in the bergschrund (it is usually

Approaching Squirrel Hill, Washburn Route. R. J. SECOR

Looking northwest from 12,500 feet on the Washburn Route. R. J. Secor

filled with snow) at the base of the West Buttress itself. The route continues southeast and heads to Windy Corner. Windy Corner is the most heavily crevassed section of the Washburn Route, and the route becomes a narrow path that turns east and then northeast, skirting the southern cliffs of the middle portion of the West Buttress while remaining above the jumbled ice on the right. Some large crevasses seem to mark the 14,000-foot contour; these are passed on their left sides, and the route continues to the campsite in Genet Basin at 14,200 feet. Strong parties can reach Genet Basin in five to six hours from 11,000 feet, but some expeditions take eight to twelve hours.

Although this camp is at 14,200 feet, it is commonly referred to as the "14,000-foot camp." Most expeditions use it as an advanced base camp and spend several days resting, acclimatizing, and drinking copious amounts of liquids, getting ready for the push on to the 17,200-foot camp and, ultimately, the South Peak. Every tent site should have its own 360-degree wind wall (as high as the tent), and many expeditions have outdoor kitchens (with windbreaks, seats with backs, and tables made out of snow). Wise climbers also construct igloos in the event that a severe storm destroys tents. Pit latrines are in place, and every climber must use these for both feces and urine. Denali National Park and Preserve has a ranger camp here to expedite rescues, provide emergency medical care, relay weather reports, and enforce the law.

Traversing Windy Corner. R. J. SECOR

The Washburn Route goes north from Genet Basin and ascends the face leading to the crest of the upper West Buttress. This face has avalanched under extreme conditions. There are lots of small and large crevasses across the lower part of this face, and many climbers make the mistake of stopping at flat spots that are, in reality, hidden crevasses. The route leads up to the bergschrund at 15,400 feet, which marks the base of the headwall, the technical crux of the route. Two fixed ropes (one for ascent, and the other for descent) are usually placed here each year by the guide concessionaires for the use of all climbers. (Don't hang off the fixed ropes; instead, climb in balance, and use the rope as an upper belay with an ascender attached to your harness.) The upper lip of the bergschrund can be up to 60 degrees in angle, but the slope above the 'schrund is a consistent 45 degrees and leads up to the crest of the upper West Buttress at 16,200 feet, commonly known as the "16,000-foot camp."

There are a few small campsites here, exposed to Denali's winds. The route turns right (east) and wanders up along the rocky, exposed crest of the upper West Buttress. There may be a few fixed ropes at some especially exposed places along the crest of the buttress. One landmark along this ridge is "Washburn's Thumb," located at approximately 16,800 feet; this is passed by a steep YDS class 2 gully on its left (north) side. This is followed by a short, exposed YDS class 3 traverse across the north side of the ridge.

Genet Basin, with Mount Foraker in the distance. R. J. Secor

Campsites in Genet Basin. R. J. SECOR

Camp in Genet Basin. R. J. SECOR

The headwall of the Washburn Route. R. J. Secor

Climbing the headwall of the Washburn Route. R. J. SECOR

Mount Foraker from the headwall of the Washburn Route. R. J. SECOR

The rock changes from solid, pink granite to loose, black slate near 17,000 feet. The route continues over the top of Point 17,230 feet and then descends to the basin at 17,200 feet, commonly known as the "17,000-foot camp." The best campsites here are along the western edge of the basin, where the rocks provide some wind protection. All tent sites should be surrounded by high, snow-block windbreaks, and igloos should also be built in case a major storm destroys tents. Strong parties can reach this campsite in four to five hours from 14,000 feet, and others may take eight to twelve hours.

The Washburn Route heads east across the basin and then makes a gradual ascending traverse up and left toward Denali Pass. Many expeditions have met their Waterloos traversing this 30- to 45-degree slope. *More climbing falls have occurred here than on any other route on Denali.* Rope up, use an ice ax (not ski poles), and employ the running belays, ascending and descending. The slope is usually in the shade in the morning, and subzero temperatures have led to frostbite. This slope has a reputation for being icy, but it has also avalanched under extreme conditions. Assess your chances of reaching the summit while climbing to Denali Pass. If you are not climbing at least 300 vertical feet per hour, turn back and spend the remainder of the day resting and drinking water and perhaps try again the next day. Turn right (south) above Denali Pass and ascend the broad, vague, left (east) side

The 17,200-foot camp, Washburn Route. R. J. Secor

Traversing to Denali Pass, Washburn Route. R. J. SECOR

Climbing the summit ridge. R. J. SECOR

The midnight sunset with Mount Foraker, Mount Hunter, and Denali. R. J. SECOR

of the ridge leading up toward Archdeacon's Tower. Many parties have gotten lost descending this slope, and it is essential that this section of the route be well wanded. This means placing one wand every 100 feet; at least 100 wands are needed from Denali Pass, or 150 wands from the 17,200 foot camp, to the summit. There is a weather sensor near 19,000 feet, located atop some rocks northwest of Archdeacon's Tower (the first one blew away in 1991). The route passes Archdeacon's Tower on its west side and descends to the Football Field, a large, flat plateau at 19,500 feet. Cross the Football Field and ascend the west side of the summit headwall to Kahiltna Horn, which marks the western end of the summit ridge. Turn left (east) and, keeping away from the cornices on the south side of the ridge, ascend the last 200 vertical feet to the apex of North America. The ascent from 17,200 feet to the summit should take from seven to ten hours, with three to five hours for the descent.

Further reading: *AAJ* (1947): 283–93; *AAJ* (1952): 212–26; *ANAM* (1961): 44–49; *ANAM* (1971): 16–17; *ANAM* (1977): 12–14, 16–17; *ANAM* (1978): 12–14; *ANAM* (1979): 21–23; *ANAM* (1980): 21–23; *ANAM* (1981): 16–21; *ANAM* (1982): 21–22, 24–28, 32–33; *ANAM* (1983): 21–22, 24–28, 32–33; *ANAM* (1984) 10–11, 17–23; *ANAM* (1985): 25–29, 34–39; *ANAM* (1986): 18–20, 22–25, 27–28; *ANAM* (1987): 27–28; *ANAM* (1988): 22–25; *ANAM* (1989): 19–27; *ANAM* (1990): 19–26, 28–29; *ANAM* (1991): 18–19; *ANAM*

(1992): 14–20; *ANAM* (1993): 19–21, 22–24, 27–28; *ANAM* (1994): 20–22, 24–27; *ANAM* (1995): 22–23, 25–27; *ANAM* (1996): 16–19, 21–22, 24–25; *ANAM* (1997): 11, 13–15, 17–19; Bradford Washburn, "Mount McKinley Conquered by New Route," *National Geographic* (August 1953): 219–48; Paul Crews, "Accident on Mount McKinley," *Summit* (August 1960): 2–7; Jim Woodfield, "Canadians Seriously Frostbitten on McKinley Ascent," *Summit* (August 1961): 8–13; Hans Metz, "To McKinley on Skis," *Summit* (November 1963): 2–5; Arlene Blum, "The Damsels and Denali," *Summit* (May 1971): 18–26; Kevin Marshman, "Death and Life on Mount McKinley," *Summit* (January–February 1984): 20–23; Jon Krakauer, "Club Denali," *Outside* (December 1987): 46–109; Art Davidson, *Minus 148°* (Seattle: Cloudcap, 1986); Colby Coombs, *Denali's West Buttress: A Climber's Guide* (Seattle: The Mountaineers, 1997).

DENNEN'S GULLY VARIATION—ALASKA GRADE 2

This variation leads to the crest of the West Buttress approximately half a mile west of where the fixed ropes end along the Washburn Route. It was first climbed on June 29, 1982, by Barney Dennen. This 1,700-foot gully is from 40 to 50 degrees in angle. Some unkind people have named this route "Dennen's Folly." While walking east along the crest of the West Buttress in a whiteout, Dennen fell when a cornice collapsed. He lost his pack and mittens in the fall and dug a small cave about 500 feet down the north side of the crest. He managed to crawl up to the fixed ropes the next day with badly frostbitten hands. The nineteen-year-old eventually lost most of his fingers.

Further reading: *ANAM* (1983): 28–29.

ROCK RIB VARIATION—ALASKA GRADE 2

The first ascent was in 1958 by Bob Elliott, Fergus O'Connor, Bruce Gilbert, Martin Mushkin, Clarence LaBell, and Ed Cooper. This party found the headwall of the Washburn Route plated with blue-green ice, so they traversed left across steep ice and ascended two rock ribs, separated by a 200-foot, 55-degree ice ridge.

Further reading: *The Mountaineer* (1959): 101–102.

RESCUE GULLY VARIATION—ALASKA GRADE 2

This 40-degree gully provides a direct route between Genet Basin and the 17,200-foot camp of the Washburn Route. As the name implies, injured or ill climbers are usually lowered down this route to salvation by rescue teams. Able-bodied mountaineers will find the Washburn Route preferable: It is easier for route-finding in a whiteout, and it offers more interesting climbing.

Further reading: *ANAM* (1997): 6–7.

RESCUE RIB VARIATION—ALASKA GRADE 2

This variation ascends the rock rib immediately to the right of Rescue Gully. It was first climbed in 1993 by Jeff Applebee and Stephen Koch. Other than one section of very loose rock, it is a good route that ends at the 17,200-foot basin of the Washburn Route.

Further reading: *AAJ* (1994): 114.

DENALI FACE VARIATION—ALASKA GRADE 2

This has also been called the Direct West Buttress. It leaves the Washburn Route just above the 17,200-foot basin. Instead of traversing to Denali Pass, it makes a direct ascent of the 30- to 40-degree face above the basin to rejoin the Washburn Route at 19,200 feet. This was first climbed by Jon Jones on June 10, 1977.

Further reading: *CAJ* (1978) 23–28.

McCLOD'S RIB—ALASKA GRADE 3

This route ascends the 4,500-foot left-hand rib of the Messner Couloir. It was climbed solo on June 10, 1977, by Bugs McKeith. The bottom part of this rib is marked by a small icefall. Cross several large crevasses to the left of the icefall and climb onto the subtle crest of the rib, marked by a few rocks sticking out from the broad 40- to 50-degree snow and ice slope. A steep rock buttress is encountered at the 16,700-foot level. Bypass this to the left by climbing a wide couloir that splits into three branches several hundred feet higher. Take the 60-degree right branch and climb back onto the crest of McClod's Rib. Follow the rib to where it merges into the summit headwall, and continue up to meet the Washburn Route at 19,200 feet.

Further reading: *AAJ* (1978): 507–8; *CAJ* (1978): 23–29.

MESSNER COULOIR—ALASKA GRADE 3

This route ascends the large, hourglass-shaped couloir on the west face of Denali. It was first *climbed* June 13, 1976, by Reinhold Messner and Oswald Olz, but it was first *skied* in 1972 by Sylvan Saudan. This 4,800-foot couloir varies from 40 to 50 degrees in angle and meets the Washburn Route immediately west of Archdeacon's Tower.

Further reading: *AAJ* (1977): 148; *ANAM* (1988): 21–23; *ANAM* (1993): 27–28.

WEST FACE—ALASKA GRADE 3

This mixed route ascends the face between the Messner Couloir and the Orient Express. It was first climbed May 17, 1991, by Miroslav Smíd. He reported rock up to YDS 5.8 and ice up to 70 degrees. The route starts by traversing up and right from the bottom of the Messner Couloir across rock, snow, and ice for six pitches, followed by easier climbing up snow and ice ramps up the subtle right-hand rib of the Messner Couloir. A direct variation of the right-hand rib was climbed in 1993 by Mark Leffler and Robert Schneider: The crux was 30 to 40 feet of vertical rock and ice.

Further reading: *AAJ* (1992): 119–20; *AAJ* (1994): 114.

ORIENT EXPRESS—ALASKA GRADE 3

This is the 4,000-foot, 35- to 45-degree couloir on the far right-hand side of the west face of Denali. It is immediately to the left of the upper part of the West Rib. More climbers have been killed here than anywhere else on Denali; climbing falls occur between 17,600 and 19,300 feet. It is unfortunate that this name has now become semiofficial: Even Denali National Park and Preserve has started to identify this route as the Orient Express. Climbers of many nations have fallen down this route due to climbing unroped or not placing running belays when roped. The first catastrophic fall occurred on June 29, 1972, and involved Mitsuko Toyama, Nobue Yajima, and Sachiko Watanabe, a group of Japanese women who were descending the West Rib. The first ascent was on June 9, 1977, by Canadians Patrick Morrow and Bernhard Ehmann, after their ascent of Reilly's Rib. Since that time, two more Japanese, five Koreans, four Britons, four Americans, a Spaniard, and a Croatian have fallen down this couloir.

Further reading: *ANAM* (1980): 19–24; *ANAM* (1983): 29–30; *ANAM* (1984): 9–10; *ANAM* (1990): 26–27; *ANAM* (1993): 24–25; *ANAM* (1996): 19–20; *ANAM* (1997): 9–10.

· CHAPTER 4 ·

Southwestern Routes

All these routes are approached via the Northeast Fork of Kahiltna Glacier, the "Valley of Death." The Northeast Fork is comparatively narrow and surrounded by hanging glaciers, and naturally occurring avalanches have been known to sweep across the entire basin. A party of four approached Cassin Ridge in 1980 via the Northeast Fork, as did a solo climber in 1987, and neither party was ever seen or heard from again. It is presumed that they died in avalanches in the Valley of Death.

The approach begins at Kahiltna Base and follows the Washburn Route down to the main fork of Kahiltna Glacier and then up the main Kahiltna Glacier for approximately 5 miles to the base of Ski Hill, at the junction of the main fork and Northeast Fork of Kahiltna Glacier. This is the usual first campsite of the Washburn Route, at 7,800 feet. The approach then goes to the right (northeast) and keeps to the left-center of the Northeast Fork, passing through several areas of crevasses (avalanche danger!) for approximately 3 1/2 miles to the bottom of the icefall at the base of the West Rib. There is a campsite in this area atop a small hill, but it provides minimal protection from avalanches. The route then goes left and ascends the left edge of the icefall to the base of the couloir, where the West Rib route starts at 11,100 feet; the campsite in this area is to the west, on the rock face, and out of the way of avalanches that sweep down the couloir. Those who continue up, bound for either the routes on the southwest face or Cassin Ridge, continue up the left side of the glacier, despite the exposure to avalanches. The safest campsite in the upper glacier is at 11,600 feet, at the far eastern end of the upper cirque, beneath Kahiltna Notch and atop a small rib. This site is usually out of the path of the huge avalanches that drop from the southwest face of Denali, but it may be exposed to some rock- and icefall from the ridge between Kahiltna Notch and the Kahiltna Peaks.

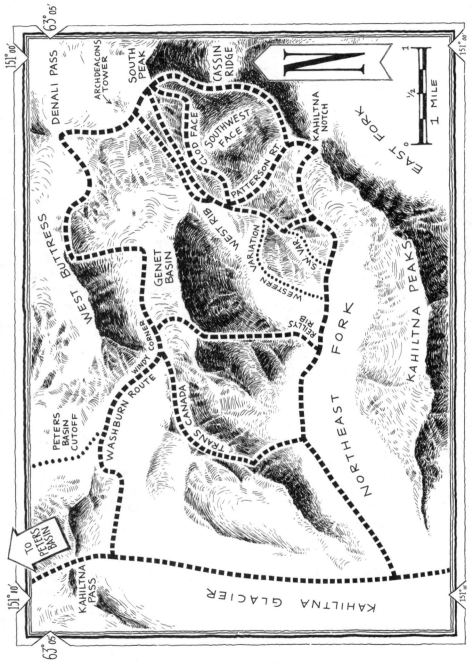

· SOUTHWESTERN ROUTES ·

TRANS CANADA—ALASKA GRADE 3

This route has also been called "Turtle Ridge." This 5,000-foot, 2½-mile-long ridge rises from the junction of the main fork and Northeast Fork of Kahiltna Glacier to meet the Washburn Route just beneath Windy Corner. It could be considered a variation to the Washburn Route, appealing to climbers seeking more than a slog up a beaten path. It was descended in June 1989 by Mugs Stump, Paul Fitzgerald, and Conrad Anker, but it was first ascended over a period of four days by Mike Kurth, Timo Saukko, Mario Bilodeau, Peter Mattsson, and Ross Cloutier on May 27, 1990. The very bottom of the ridge is somewhat jumbled and is bypassed by ascending the Northeast Fork of Kahiltna Glacier to the 9,000-foot level at the base of the Canada Couloir. This twelve-pitch, 50-degree couloir (exposed to rock-fall) leads to the crest of the ridge above the broken section; it is exited by means of a rock move. Snow slopes (with hidden crevasses) lead up to the mixed, knife-edged, and corniced ridge leading to Point 12,960 feet, and steeper slopes continue to the top of Point 13,300 feet. The traverse to Point 13,350 feet is narrow and corniced, followed by a short descent to Windy Corner.

Further reading: *AAJ* (1991): 154-55; *CAJ* (1991): 87–88.

REILLY'S RIB—ALASKA GRADE 4

This route has also been called the West Rim. It ascends the prominent 4,000-foot, mile-long rib rising above the middle of the Northeast Fork of Kahiltna Glacier. It was first climbed over a period of three days by Bernhard Ehmann and Patrick Morrow in May 1977, followed almost immediately by their rivals Mike Helms and Reilly Moss. Turn left beneath the icefall and cross the flat glacier to the base of the rib. The climbing starts with mixed rock and snow climbing to the 35-degree crest of the rib, followed for fifteen pitches to a campsite at 11,000 feet, immediately above a short, steep ice pitch. Above this point, the first ascent party encountered an area of delicate cornices, overcome with the aid of psychological belays anchored in honeycombed snow. This is followed by several ice pitches that end with a 60-degree ice ramp, leading to the more gentle upper slopes of the rib. From the top of Reilly's Rib, the route goes north, meeting the Washburn Route at the 13,600-foot level, above Windy Corner.

Further reading: *AAJ* (1978): 505; *CAJ* (1978): 28–29.

West Buttress from Kahiltna Dome. BRIAN OKONEK, ALASKA-DENALI GUIDING

Northeast Fork Kahiltna Glacier. Brian Okonek, Alaska-Denali Guiding

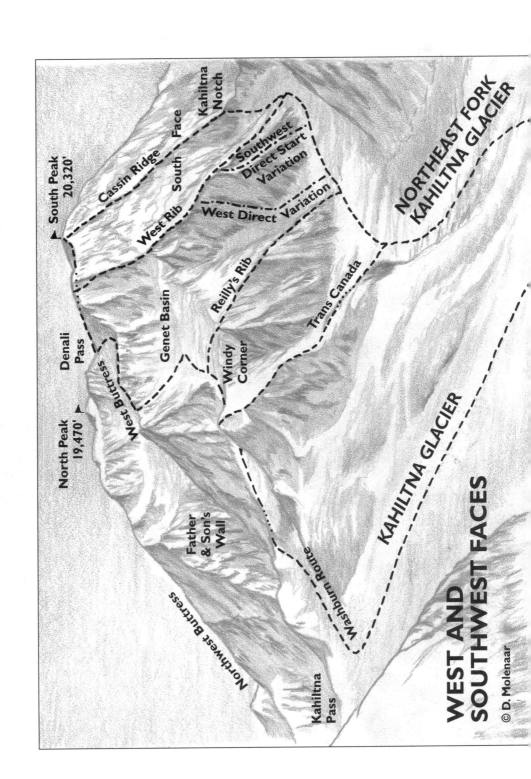

South Peak 20,320'

Cassin Ridge

South Face

Kahiltna Notch

Southwest Direct Start Variation

West Rib South

West Direct Variation

Reilly's Rib

Genet Basin

Trans Canada

Denali Pass

Windy Corner

West Buttress

North Peak 19,470'

NORTHEAST FORK KAHILTNA GLACIER

Father & Son's Wall

KAHILTNA GLACIER

Northwest Buttress

Washburn Route

Kahiltna Pass

WEST AND SOUTHWEST FACES

© D. Molenaar

WEST RIB—ALASKA GRADE 4

The West Rib of the southwest face rises 4,500 feet in a little more than a mile, and the upper part of this route climbs 3,900 feet, also in a little more than a mile, to meet the Washburn Route at the Football Field just below the top of the South Peak. It is a popular technical route, not as severe as Cassin Ridge on the south face. It was first climbed over a period of twelve days by Pete Sinclair, Jake Breitenbach, Barry Corbet, and Bill Buckingham in June 1959. The first winter ascent was achieved by Charles Sassara and Robert Frank on March 11, 1983. The route starts by ascending a couloir on the southeast side of the rib. This is the crux of the climb, and the 1,200-foot, 40- to 50-degree snow/ice couloir leads to the crest of the rib. Ascend the corniced rib for a few hundred feet to a campsite on a snow ledge that is left of the crest at 12,300 feet. Continue up the crest, overcoming the first ice dome at 12,400 feet, followed by the second ice dome at approximately 13,500 feet (a possible campsite). The slope angles ease above the second dome. Follow the rib crest to 14,000 feet, at the bottom of a rock spur. Overcome the bergschrund and continue up difficult rock, followed by a 500-foot ice couloir to a campsite at 14,800 feet. Mixed climbing then leads to the top of the rib at 15,300 feet, overlooking Genet Basin and the Washburn Route.

The West Rib route turns right and climbs rock and snow along the crest of this upper ridge to an exposed campsite at 16,500 feet (some parties move to the left and camp in a crevasse for wind protection). There is another exposed campsite at 16,900 feet. The route continues up the ridge to where it ends at a broad snow slope at approximately 18,000 feet. (The couloir that drops off to the left is the Orient Express; the sixteen climbers who have been killed in climbing falls down the Orient Express have fallen between 17,600 and 19,300 feet.) The West Rib route goes up and left across this broad snow slope to the left-hand upper couloir. This 40- to 50-degree couloir ends at 19,500 feet, where a short walk to the east leads to the Washburn Route as it crosses the Football Field immediately below the summit. Most parties descend to the Washburn Route from the 16,000-foot level rather than descend the entire West Rib route.

Further reading: *AAJ* (1960): 1–9; *ANAM* (1971): 15–16; *ANAM* (1979): 21–22; *ANAM* (1982): 27; *ANAM* (1983): 18–20, 24; *ANAM* (1984): 16–17; *ANAM* (1986): 21–22; *ANAM* (1991): 21–22; *ANAM* (1994): 22–26; *ANAM* (1995): 27–28.

WESTERN DIRECT START VARIATION—ALASKA GRADE 4

This variation to the West Rib was climbed in June 1972 by Sueko Inoue, Mitsuko Toyama, Michiko Sekita, Nobue Yajima, and Sachiko Watanabe. It ascends the deep ice couloir on the west side of the West Rib to its crest at 13,000 feet.

SOUTHWESTERN DIRECT START VARIATION—ALASKA GRADE 2

This was first climbed in 1977 by a party from the Hosei University Alpine Club. It ascends the mixed couloir on the southwest side of the West Rib.

WEST RIB FROM GENET BASIN VARIATION—ALASKA GRADE 3

This is the most common variation done on the West Rib. Head southeast from the 14,200-foot camp of the Washburn Route across Genet Basin to the upper part of the West Rib, meeting it between 15,500 and 16,500 feet. Some big crevasses must be crossed in the upper part of Genet Basin, but there are no other obstacles, except for the hazards of climbing to 20,000 feet in a sub-arctic latitude. This variation was first done on August 8, 1975, by Masaaki Hatakeyama, Akio Shoji, and Teruzo Nakamura.

PATTERSON ROUTE—ALASKA GRADE 4

This route has also been called the "Wickwire Variation," but it has been named here in memory of Leif-Norman Patterson. It can be considered a variation of the West Rib, but it touches the original 1959 route for only a short distance near 14,000 feet. It was first climbed over a three-and-a-half-day period on June 25, 1972, by Jim Wickwire, Alex Bertulis, Thomas Stewart, Robert Schaller, Charles Raymond, and Leif-Norman Patterson, after an initial two-week attempt on Cassin Ridge. The route ascends the east-facing glacier that curves into the cirque formed by Cassin Ridge, the southwest face, and the east spur of the West Rib. The climbing starts directly opposite the Japanese Couloir of Cassin Ridge. Bypass the seracs, crevasses, and ice cliffs near the bottom of this glacier. Relatively easy climbing (but exposed to avalanches from the hanging glacier looming overhead) leads up the center of the glacier to a broad snowfield at 14,000 feet with hidden crevasses. From here, the route goes straight up the gradually steepening slope, staying close to the rocks on the right and avoiding the potential avalanche slopes on the left. Eventually, a short ice pitch is met, followed by mixed snow and rock scrambling to a comfortable ledge at 16,800 feet, at the bottom of the prominent hourglass couloir. Ascend the 700-foot, 40- to 45-degree ice and hard snow couloir to a boulder-strewn shoulder at 17,800 feet. This is followed by a steepening 1,600-foot snow slope that ends at the southwestern end of the Football Field. Go to the right, and ascend the Washburn Route up to Kahiltna Horn and on to the summit.

West Rib. BRIAN OKONEK, ALASKA-DENALI GUIDING

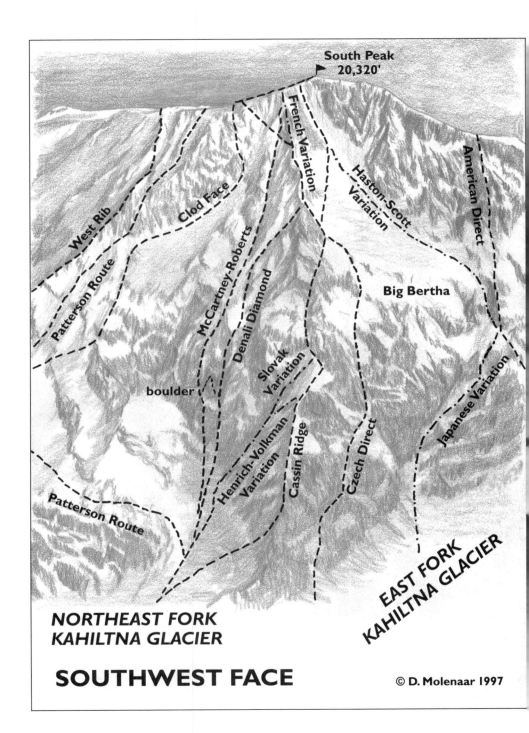

South Peak
20,320'

French Variation

Haston-Scott Variation

American Direct

West Rib

Clod Face

McCartney-Roberts

Denali Diamond

Big Bertha

Patterson Route

Slovak Variation

boulder

Japanese Variation

Henrich-Volkman Variation

Cassin Ridge

Czech Direct

Patterson Route

NORTHEAST FORK KAHILTNA GLACIER

EAST FORK KAHILTNA GLACIER

SOUTHWEST FACE

© D. Molenaar 1997

Further reading: *AAJ* (1973): 282–88; Alex Bertulis, "Mount McKinley's South Face, Alpine Style," *Mountain* 28 (July 1973): 24–29.

CLOD FACE—ALASKA GRADE 4

This route ascends the upper 5,500 feet of the southwest face of Denali. Aside from two short rock sections (at 15,700 and 19,500 feet), most of the climbing is on snow or ice of 40 to 50 degrees. It was first climbed over a period of eight days on June 3, 1977, by Bugs McKeith, Eckhart Grassman, Jon Jones, and Allan Derbyshire. Go up and right from the 14,000-foot level of the West Rib, traversing between two prominent bergschrunds to reach the crest of a small rock rib at the 15,000-foot level. Ascend the crest of this rib, past a short mixed step at 15,700 feet, to where it merges with the higher snow slope at 16,200 feet. From the top of the rib, climb up and right across mixed slopes to the bottom of a steep rock buttress at 17,000 feet. Traverse almost horizontally to the right, keeping beneath the rock face and above the hanging glacier high in the middle of the southwest face, and then make a right diagonal ascent to the top of the glacier at 17,800 feet. Move to the right across a rock shoulder and then into a small couloir. In fact, there are many couloirs that link together and lead up the face to the Football Field, immediately beneath the summit. The first ascent party kept to the right side of the face and aimed for the far right-hand side of a cornice, visible on the skyline. A 100-foot rock and ice chimney leads up the right side of this cornice to the Football Field.

Further reading: *AAJ* (1978): 507; *CAJ* (1978): 23–28.

MCCARTNEY-ROBERTS ROUTE—ALASKA GRADE 5

This extreme route ascends the true southwest face of Denali. It was first climbed in June 1980 by Simon McCartney and Jack Roberts, but this party's separation, descent, and rescue became a bigger story than the ascent route, and it is regrettable that more details are not available on what may be the most difficult route yet climbed on Denali.

The climb starts from the center of the southwest face and leads to the snowfield beneath the "large boulder" located approximately halfway up the rock band. The first ascent party took two and a half days to reach this landmark. The route then goes left before attacking the headwall, which features sustained YDS 5.8 climbing. A ramp on an overhanging wall eventually ends beneath another overhang, and the Roberts Traverse passes this by means of 5.9 rock climbing. The route ends by ascending the couloir to the right of Clod Face and meets Cassin Ridge at 19,500 feet.

Further reading: *Mountain* 75 (September–October 1980): 14–15; *ANAM* (1981): 24–28.

DENALI DIAMOND—ALASKA GRADE 5

This is another extreme route on the southwest face that lacks details. It was first climbed June 10, 1983, over a period of seventeen days (with eight days of storm) by Rolf Graage and Bryan Becker. It starts to the right of the McCartney-Roberts Route. The route involves thirty-seven and a half pitches, including an A3 rope length over a 25-foot roof. The most difficult climbing on the route is the last two and a half pitches to the top of the lower rock wall, which took two days to complete. Low-angled ice fields then lead to upper Cassin Ridge, which is followed to the summit. Like the McCartney-Roberts Route, this is a contender for the most difficult route done on the mountain.

Further reading: *AAJ* (1984): 84–86; *ANAM* (1984): 18–19.

• CHAPTER 5 •

Southern Routes

All these routes are (or can be) approached from the East Fork of Kahiltna Glacier. The approach begins by going west from Kahiltna Base, dropping down to the main fork of Kahiltna Glacier, and heading north for approximately 2 ½ miles, past Sled Hill, to the junction with the East Fork. Turn right (east) and keep to the left-center side of the glacier for approximately 5 miles to an icefall near 9,500 feet. Pass this icefall on its extreme left side to avoid possible avalanches from the South Buttress. Continue ascending the left side of the East Fork, passing the major icefall between 10,000 and 11,000 feet on its left side. Most parties establish their advance base camps at 11,200 feet in a protected spot either beneath or just beyond the couloir leading to Kahiltna Notch.

Although the East Fork of Kahiltna Glacier is not as dangerous as the Northeast Fork, it is still exposed to avalanche hazards. The first dangerous location is between the 9,000- and 9,400-foot levels of the glacier, a narrow spot where avalanches from the Kahiltna Peaks and the extreme southern end of the South Buttress of Denali have been known to cover almost the entire width of the glacier. Perhaps the most famous avalanche hazard is the hanging glacier high on the middle of the South Face of Denali, dubbed "Big Bertha." A team of three Japanese climbers disappeared in the cirque high on the East Fork, and underneath Big Bertha, in July 1981. There are many potential hazards from the upper part of the South Buttress as well. Campsites must be selected with care, and climbers must not loiter under dangerous spots.

Further reading: *ANAM* (1977): 14; *ANAM* (1982): 29–32.

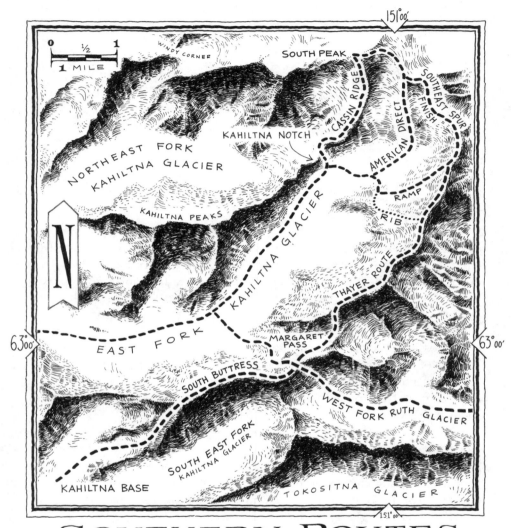

◆ SOUTHERN ROUTES ◆

CASSIN RIDGE—ALASKA GRADE 5

Cassin Ridge is one of the most coveted big mountain routes in the world. It gains 9,000 feet over a distance of 2 miles, topping out very close to the summit of the South Peak of Denali. It was first climbed on July 19, 1961, over a period of twenty-six days by Ricardo Cassin, Romano Perego, Luigi Airoldi, Giancarlo Canali, Luigi Alippi, and Annibale Zucchi. The first winter ascent (and the second winter ascent of Denali itself) was achieved by Jonathan Waterman, Roger Mear, and Michael Young on March 6, 1982. The description that follows is a mixture of the variations established by subsequent parties, representing the current route, which bypasses some of Ricardo Cassin's original pitches.

Cassin Ridge can be approached from either the northeast or the east fork of Kahiltna Glacier. Most parties use the Northeast Fork, despite the real danger from avalanches and the sincere admonitions of Denali National Park and Preserve rangers. Although the East Fork of Kahiltna Glacier is a bit longer, it is the safest approach (see the introduction to chapter 4). Leave the East Fork of Kahiltna Glacier at 11,000 feet and climb the narrow, 1,000-foot, 60-degree couloir leading to Kahiltna Notch (first climbed in July 1967 by Boyd Everett, Bill Phillips, Del Langbauer, Clarence Serfoss, and James Underwood). Then go to the right (north) and traverse the spectacular 400-foot knife-edge ridge crest to the top of the Cassin Couloir; there is small tent site about 100 feet short of the top. Instead of climbing the rock and ice face above the couloir (as Cassin did), rappel 300 feet down to the upper snowfield of the Northeast Fork of Kahiltna Glacier. Traverse north for a few hundred feet to the base of the Japanese Couloir (first climbed in May 1967 by Kasaku Keira, Akio Kawagoe, Masahiro Shukin, Yoshitaka Akimoto, Koichi Hirakawa, Tsukasa Yamanaka, Hideki Ujiie, and Takao Sasaki).

Although there are more difficult pitches higher on the route, the 1,000-foot Japanese Couloir is widely regarded as the objective crux of Cassin Ridge, due to its consistent difficulties and exposure to falling rock and ice. It starts with three pitches of 45-degree ice climbing to the rock on the left side of the couloir. Climb easy rock and ice to a vertical rock wall. Bypass this by going to the right, underneath the wall, and then climb steep ice mixed with rock to another rock wall. This is overcome by means of a 50-foot rock chimney (YDS 5.2 to 5.4), followed immediately by going up and to the right through a narrow V-shaped chimney over ice to easier ground and a good ledge (Cassin's original route comes in from the right at this point). Climb diagonally left back into the main couloir and ascend the left side, with occasional moves onto YDS class 4 rock, where the couloir narrows. The last pitch can either climb rotten YDS class 4 rock to the left or ascend 60-degree ice on the right. The top of the Japanese Couloir is at 13,400 feet and is marked by Cassin Ledge (a bad joke: it is actually tilted, jumbled boulders).

Go to the right around the overhanging rock above Cassin Ledge and climb 45-degree ice between rocks to the top of a rock cliff. Traverse to the right along the top edge of the rock cliff to the base of the Chimney Pitch: 10 feet wide, 50 feet high, YDS 5.2 to 5.5. From the top of the chimney, climb diagonally right over exposed rock and ice to the highest big boulder. Next, climb an ever-steepening snow and ice slope up and left to the crest of the Ice Rib. Continue up the exposed Ice Rib to approximately 14,000 feet. If Cassin Ledge is a bad joke, then the overhanging crevasse that appeared here in the mid-1980s is a cruel one. (There was once an ancient fixed rope stretched across both sides of this Blue Meanie, tight as a banjo string.) This, the ice crux of the Cassin, is passed on its left side, first by rappelling into the gap, and then by traversing up and across vertical blue ice for 300 feet to the upper side of the crevasse—easier said than done. Continue up the now relatively easy glacier to the First Rock Band, aiming for the only apparent break in this cliff.

The First Rock Band is guarded by a small cliff at its base. This is over-come by a YDS class 4 crack, 10 feet to the left of a small overhang. Thirty feet above is another short vertical wall, YDS 5.2 to 5.6, that leads to a snow and ice ramp that goes to the right. Climb this ramp for 300 feet, and then go to the left and climb a right-facing inside corner, with vertical ice and some YDS 5.1 rock. From the top of this corner, traverse to the right for 20 feet over three boulders and climb a short rock face (YDS 5.1 to 5.6). A 60-degree ice face then leads up for 75 feet to the base of a right-facing, ver-tical inside corner. Climb the 80-foot corner (YDS 5.1 to 5.4), and then go to the right over mixed snow and rock to a small 8-foot chimney, followed by more traversing to the right for another 100 feet to the base of a major verti-cal rock wall: the Rib Pitch. The Rib Pitch is widely considered the rock crux of Cassin Ridge. It would probably be rated YDS 5.4 in Joshua Tree on a sunny day in rock-climbing shoes, but at 15,500 feet on the south face of the apex of North America at a subarctic latitude, few climbers rate it at less than YDS 5.8, and it seldom goes completely free. From the top of the Rib Pitch, go up and right over easier mixed snow, ice, and rock to a large boul-der, and continue up the ridge to a campsite at 15,700 feet.

Go to the left across easy snow and rock to the Second Rock Band. Climb this wall via an almost hidden 300-foot rock chimney (steep, but with excel-lent holds; YDS 5.1 to 5.2). The Third Rock Band is above the top of the couloir. Cassin climbed this directly, but a faster and easier alternative (first climbed by the Japanese in 1967) is to traverse to the right for 300 feet across snow to the bottom of an outside corner at the base of the Third Rock Band. Go around the corner and ascend another 200 feet over snow to the base of more steep rock. Traverse up and right for several hundred feet, avoiding all rock, to the prominent snowfield on the south face above Big Bertha. Climb the snowfield for about 800 vertical feet, keeping within 200 feet of the ridge crest to the left. Ascend a long, easy snow couloir back left to the crest of Cassin Ridge at 17,700 feet, where there is a campsite. Climb the left side of the ridge for 500 feet before climbing onto its crest. Traverse to the left for 200 feet, over rock at first, then across a small couloir, and then climb 200 feet over mixed snow and rock to a small ledge at the base of a large (40-foot) boulder—another campsite. Leave the ridge crest here and go up and left, across the bases of several snow couloirs (these have been climbed to the top of Kahiltna Horn under ideal conditions) to the southern edge of the Football Field. Turn right, ascend the west ridge of Kahiltna Horn, and continue on to the summit of Denali.

Cassin's party descended the route, but most parties today climb Cassin Ridge in alpine style and descend the Washburn Route back to Kahiltna Base. This also gives them the opportunity to pick up gear or rubbish cached at the 14,000-foot level of the Washburn Route during the acclimatization period.

Further reading: *AAJ* (1962): 27–37; *AAJ* (1968): 10–20, 118–120; *AAJ* (1983): 93–97; *AAJ* (1997): 173; *ANAM* (1975): 7; *ANAM* (1983): 33–34; *ANAM* (1987): 28–31; *ANAM* (1988): 24–25; *ANAM* (1989): 25–26, 28–29; *ANAM* (1990): 27–28; *ANAM* (1993): 21–22; Matt Culberson, "In the Eye of the Beholder," *Climbing* 134 (October–November 1992): 62–69, 132–35.

CASSIN COULOIR—ALASKA GRADE 5

This is the route followed by Ricardo Cassin's expedition on the first ascent of Cassin Ridge. The Cassin Couloir is approximately 600 feet to the right (north) of the Kahiltna Notch Couloir. The 1,200-foot, 60-degree couloir is exposed to rockfall, however, and the Kahiltna Notch Couloir is the preferred route.

Ascend the right side of the Cassin Couloir for approximately 300 feet to a large rock overhang. Climb the edge of the rocks (to avoid rockfall) for another 300 feet, and then climb the ice for four pitches to where the couloir narrows. Climb the right side of the couloir for two pitches between the ice and the rock. The couloir is very narrow at this point. Traverse left, across the couloir, and climb the rock on the left side of the couloir for one pitch. The next two pitches are difficult rock (UIAA IV+), followed by an overhanging rock face (UIAA V+). The couloir ends with one more pitch over ice.

From the top of the Cassin Couloir, Cassin's party traversed to the left and climbed the rock along the right side of the upper part of the Japanese Couloir. Traverse left and down from the ice arête that marks the top of the Cassin Couloir. After one pitch, climb up a short 20-foot face, and then traverse left for 200 feet across an ice slope to a rock face. Continue traversing across the rock for 70 feet, and then climb up and left for a pitch over mixed rock and ice (UIAA IV) to the base of some smooth granite slabs. Continue left along the base of these slabs for another pitch, and then climb the slabs directly for one more pitch (UIAA IV to V) to some wide ledges, covered with ice. Two more mixed pitches lead straight up to a ledge under a huge, pink granite overhang. Go left, ascend a short ice couloir, and continue left around an enormous boulder to the base of a large, smooth, overhanging dihedral. Another pitch of the unholy trinity of mixed climbing (ice and rock with some aid moves) leads left to the Japanese Couloir.

Further reading: *AAJ* (1962): 27–37; *AAJ* (1968): 10–20, 118–20.

FRENCH VARIATION—ALASKA GRADE 5
This variation could be called the "Upper Direct Cassin Ridge." Instead of traversing to the left toward the Football Field from the 18,500-foot level, it climbs a couloir that leads up and right to the crest of the upper Cassin Ridge. (This couloir avoids the steepest part of the upper Cassin Ridge.) The ridge crest is then followed to Kahiltna Horn, where a right turn and another 200 feet of gain lead to the South Peak of Denali. It was first climbed July 23, 1971, over a period of twenty-two days by Daniéle Germain, Bernard Germain, Benoit Renard, Vincent Renard, Yves Morin, and Michel Berquet.

Further reading: *AAJ* (1972): 56–58.

HENRICH-VOLKMAN VARIATION—ALASKA GRADE 5
This variation was discovered in one of the finest traditions of mountaineering: The first ascent party was off-route. In 1983, Wade Henrich and Roger Volkman walked past the Japanese Couloir for approximately 200 yards and climbed a long 50-degree ice slope near the edge of Denali's southwest face. This was followed by a 170-foot rock band (YDS 5.9, A1) before climbing onto the hanging glacier at the 14,000-foot level of Cassin Ridge. This 2,000-foot variation took the pair more than forty hours of continuous climbing (there were no camp or bivouac sites), exposed to falling ice from the hanging glacier above.

South Face. BRIAN OKONEK, ALASKA-DENALI GUIDING

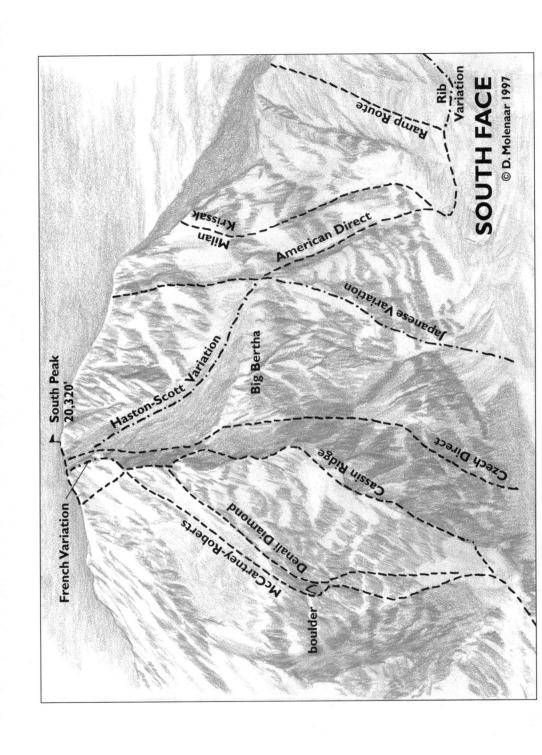

SOUTH FACE

© D. Molenaar 1997

Rib Variation

Ramp Route

Milan Krissak

American Direct

Japanese Variation

South Peak 20,320'

Haston-Scott Variation

Big Bertha

Czech Direct

French Variation

Cassin Ridge

McCartney-Roberts

Denali Diamond

boulder

SLOVAK VARIATION—ALASKA GRADE 5

This could be considered a variation of the Henrich-Volkman Variation. It was climbed in 1991 by Josef Nezerka and Zolo Demján. They started climbing about 150 feet to the left of the Henrich-Volkman line, encountering difficult mixed climbing (up to YDS 5.9 rock) and long sections of 60-degree ice. This lower face offered only hanging bivouacs or small ledges hacked out of ice. Instead of climbing directly onto the hanging glacier, they climbed the face to its left before climbing onto this glacier and meeting the Cassin Route at the 15,400-foot level.

Further reading: *AAJ* (1992): 117–19.

SOUTHWEST FACE TRAVERSE VARIATION—ALASKA GRADE 4

This traverse was first completed on May 15, 1990, by Michael Covington, Greg Smith, Bill Pierson, Joel Butler, Anatoli Boukreev, and Tim Maryon. They left Cassin Ridge at the 17,700-foot level and crossed exposed slopes from 40 to 60 degrees for more than forty pitches to the 16,300-foot level of the West Rib, under threat of potential avalanches. At first glance, this may appear to be an escape route off Cassin Ridge for a weak or injured party. But it is not a safe escape route and should be attempted only during good weather with perfect snow conditions. It has more belayed pitches than climbing to the summit via Cassin Ridge itself from 17,700 feet, so the only safe escape route off Cassin Ridge is to either climb to the summit or descend Cassin Ridge. Two climbers were killed attempting this route during severe weather, only three weeks after it was first done. In 1994, Dirk Collins and Stephen Koch took advantage of excellent snow conditions and reversed this traverse. Starting from Genet Basin, they climbed to 16,500 feet on the West Rib and crossed the southwest face to the big couloir marking the end of the McCartney-Roberts Route, which they followed to the upper Cassin Ridge and then on to the summit. They were back in Genet Basin after seventeen hours.

Further reading: *AAJ* (1991): 151, 155; *AAJ* (1994): 114; *ANAM* (1991): 16–18.

CZECH DIRECT—ALASKA GRADE 5

Although this extreme route keeps to the left of Big Bertha, it is still exposed to ice- and rockfall from Cassin Ridge. It was first climbed over a period of eleven days by Tono Krizo, Frantisek Korl, and Blazej Adam on May 23, 1984. The route starts on the left side of a rock wall topped by a small hanging glacier on the left side of the south face. It climbs through the large benches and then on top of the hanging glacier to the base of the major rock face. The route at first ascends the left side of the face and then tends to the right, skirting the left side of Big Bertha. The climbing on the face is UIAA IV to V+, with 60- to 90-degree ice. The first ascent party placed 150 rock pitons and 40 ice pitons. Ascend the snow slopes high on the south face before climbing the wide couloir to the right of Cassin Ridge, ending on the ridge between Kahiltna Horn and the South Peak. This route lacks adequate tent sites, and the first ascent party had open bivouacs.

Further reading: *AAJ* (1985): 174–75.

AMERICAN DIRECT—ALASKA GRADE 5

This route is also known as "The Centennial Wall," as the first ascent was made as part of Alaska's celebration of one hundred years as part of the United States. It has sustained difficulties, with considerable exposure to objective dangers. It was first climbed August 4, 1967, over twenty-eight days (with thirteen days of storm) by Roman Laba, Dave Seidman, Gray Thompson, and Denny Eberl.

From the base of Kahiltna Notch on the East Fork of Kahiltna Glacier, walk quickly (avalanche danger!) beneath the south face for approximately 1 mile. The lower part of the route ascends several ice chutes that are to the right of the obtuse rock and ice rib on the right side of the south face. Cross the bergschrund at 12,700 feet, and climb the 50-degree snow and ice face above. Climb straight up for 400 feet and then go diagonally left over steepening ice to the base of a rock wall. The first ascent party camped here at "Lunch Rock," a site underneath an overhanging rock at 13,200 feet.

Skirt the rock face above Lunch Rock on its left side, cross a small avalanche gully, continue up and left, and then cross a large avalanche gully. Climb 50- to 60-degree snow to the left of a rock tower. Climb to the top of the rock tower, and then go straight up 50- to 60-degree ice ribs for five pitches. Traverse left over 50-degree snow through an avalanche gully past the bottom of a vertical rock face. Fifty feet beyond the face, climb 65-degree ice to "Bleak House," the first ascent party's second camp at 14,000 feet, a narrow ledge that was hacked out underneath a vertical rock wall.

Traverse to the left for 200 feet on a narrow snow ledge that is underneath an overhanging wall, and continue straight up a 60-degree ice gully, with some YDS class 4 rock barriers. Then go up and left for 600 feet over 50- to 60-degree ice, keeping to the right side of a large avalanche chute. Cross this chute at its narrowest point, hopefully on snow, followed by 10 feet of rock. This leads to a poorly defined, rocky couloir system. Ascend this couloir system by going up and left across mixed ice (to 65 degrees) and YDS class 4 rock for nine pitches to a snow shoulder at 15,000 feet, dubbed "Spiral Camp" by the first ascent party. Traverse to the left into "Spiral Couloir" and climb it for five pitches, mostly on 45-degree snow with rock on its side. This is followed by 300 feet of 30-degree snow and easy rock scrambling to "Dartmouth Meadows," a campsite at 15,600 feet; this snow shelf in a rock corner is big enough for two tents.

The first ascent party called the next 1,500 feet of the route "The Meadows." Easy mixed snow and rock lead to the First Buttress, a major rock barrier (the first ascent party camped at its base at 16,800 feet). Traverse 300 feet to the right to a 500-foot snow fan, topped by a prominent cleft in the First Buttress. Climb through The Cleft: The first pitch requires some direct aid (YDS 5.7, A2), followed by three YDS 5.5 to 5.7 and four YDS class 4 pitches on excellent rock. These lead to the top of the First Buttress at 17,700 feet.

The first ascent party later found that The Cleft could be bypassed, and they used the following route for load carrying: From the bottom of the First Buttress, traverse up and left for several hundred feet over easy snow. Continue up through rock on another snow face for several hundred feet, gradually moving back to the right to the top of the First Buttress at 17,700 feet.

From the top of the First Buttress, traverse to the right for 400 feet, passing above the "End the War in Vietnam Pinnacle" and through a snow bowl to the right side of the Second Buttress. Bypass this on its right side by climbing 100 feet of mixed rock and snow, and then rappel only 20 feet into a small couloir. Climb this couloir diagonally to the right, with 45-degree snow and some YDS class 4 rock. This leads to a large snow couloir. Ascend the left side of this couloir (rock and snow) to the top of the Second Buttress. Easy snow climbing then leads to a large, flat campsite at 18,400 feet, at the base of the Third Buttress.

The Third Buttress is bypassed on its left side. Traverse to the left for 300 feet, passing under a large overhanging boulder. Climb diagonally right, over a 700-foot, 30-degree snow and rock face to a snow chute that leads up and right to the top of the Third Buttress, approximately 300 feet beneath the summit ridge. Climb 100 feet over 45-degree snow toward the huge cornice on the summit ridge. Traverse to the right over 60-degree snow, and either climb over or tunnel through the cornice at its weakest point (the first ascent party popped out onto the summit ridge at 19,100 feet). Turn left and follow the ridge up to the summit of the South Peak.

The first ascent party descended the South Buttress, where its support party was climbing. The most reasonable descent route these days is via the Washburn Route.

Further reading: *AAJ* (1968): 10–20; Gray Thompson, "McKinley's Centennial Wall," *Summit* (March 1968): 2–11; *Ascent* (1968): 18–21; *ANAM* (1982): 29–32.

JAPANESE VARIATION—ALASKA GRADE 5

This variation ascends a ramp system that is to the left of the obtuse rock rib of the American Direct Route. It is exposed to avalanches from Big Bertha, however, making this variation extremely hazardous. It was first climbed on July 14, 1977, over a period of twenty-two days by Kichitaka Kimura, Yushichi Senda, Mitsuo Yamaura, Tamae Watanabe, and Yuji Tsuneto. They met the American Direct Route between the Spiral Couloir and the First Buttress.

Further reading: *AAJ* (1978): 504.

HASTON-SCOTT VARIATION—ALASKA GRADE 5

This variation of the American Direct Route climbs the snowfield and the face immediately beneath the summit of the South Peak. It was first climbed in a single seven-day push by Dougal Haston and Doug Scott on May 12, 1976. It leaves the American Direct Route below the First Buttress and traverses up and left across the top of Big Bertha. It then climbs straight up the 55- to 60-degree ice face onto the summit ridge between Kahiltna Horn and the true summit.

Further reading: *AAJ* (1977): 88–95; *AAJ* (1983): 87–92; *ANAM* (1983): 20–21; *ANAM* (1992): 18–19; *Mountain* 52 (November–December 1976): 18–21.

MILAN KRISSAK MEMORIAL ROUTE—ALASKA GRADE 5

This route ascends the right side of the south face of Denali, in the area between the American Direct and the Southeast Spur Finish. It was first climbed after a five-day effort by Michal Orolin, Daniel Bakos, Vladimir Petrik, and Philip Johnson; they summited on Friday, June 13, 1980. The climbing starts by ascending a steep ice slope to a small rock band. A pitch of rock climbing leads to its right side, where an ice ramp leads steeply up and left; the first ascent party hacked out its first bivouac site along this ramp. Go to the far left-hand edge of the ramp, where it ends in a broad ice field. Keep to the right side of this ice field before heading left, aiming for an obvious break in a big rock band. Two pitches of rock lead up the break, followed by a dull snow ridge at the base of a big snowfield; the first ascent party bivouacked on a large boulder at its base. The route continues up this dull ridge to its head and then moves to the right, up a couloir, marked by a gendarme at its top. The couloir leads to the crest of the Southeast Spur Finish, and the remainder of that route is followed to the summit.

This route is named in memory of one of Czechoslovakia's outstanding mountaineers, who was killed in a helicopter crash in the High Tatras mountains during a rescue mission in June 1979.

Further reading: *AAJ* (1981): 8–14.

MASCIOLI'S PILLAR—ALASKA GRADE 5

The first ascent was accomplished June 16, 1997, by Steve House and Steve Swenson. This route ascends the right side of the 3,000-foot rock buttress that is to the left of the Ramp Route. The first ascent party climbed this route in a little more than thirty hours round-trip, including a three-hour sitting bivouac under an overhang to the left of the bottom of the Chimney Pitch. Aside from the gully and snowfield on the bottom half of the route, this route lacks natural bivouac sites.

Start by climbing the 50- to 75-degree broad ice gully to the base of the first rock band. A 120-foot YDS 5.10 pitch up an inside corner is followed by a short chimney. The first ascent party used a 200-foot rope, and the next pitch was a full rope length of YDS 5.10 with some aid moves just below the first ice field. Ascend the 50-degree ice field to the base of the prominent inside corner system on the right side of the pillar. Climb a 6-inch-wide, ice-filled crack, passing through a small roof (strenuous, YDS 5.10), and continue up poor rock (the only bad rock on the entire route) to a belay stance on a huge rock horn. This is followed by 60 feet of narrow, thin, and steep ice climbing to an easy gully. Continue up the gully, bypassing the difficult rock steps on their left sides on good rock (YDS 5.8), ending with a short, strenuous rock step at the top of the gully (20 feet, YDS 5.9) at the base of the Chimney Pitch. Go straight up the deep chimney (stemming, YDS 5.8 to 5.9, with ice deep in the crack) to a stance in an alcove. Next, traverse to the right on a flake (YDS 5.8) to a good ledge system, and then overcome a short wall (YDS 5.9). Continue up a 40-degree snow and ice ramp to the top of the chimney. The Z Pitch starts by ascending easy 45-degree ice, then traverses horizontally to the right (YDS 5.6) to more easy ice. Go straight up a 45-degree ice ramp, and after 80 feet, go to the left across the top of the large chimney system in the middle of the pillar; this was attempted earlier and later rappelled by the first ascent party. Head up and to the right to an 80-degree ice chimney; at the top, stem the chimney and then step to the left and climb 30 feet of YDS 5.8 rock to a large belay ledge. Go straight up from the ledge in an awkward inside corner (YDS 5.7) to a snowy ramp, and follow it to a short rock headwall (YDS 5.10) with ledges to a belay stance in a corner. A 30-foot, awkward YDS 5.10 dihedral leads to more ledges and the top of the hard climbing. Another 400 feet of snow and ice with some short YDS class 5 moves leads to the top of the pillar.

The logical conclusion to this route is to continue to the summit of the South Peak via the Southeast Spur Finish or to descend the Ramp Route on the South Buttress. But the first ascent party down-climbed Mascioli's Pillar to the top of the hard climbing and then rappelled to the top of the Z Pitch, followed by more rappels down the large chimney system in the middle of the pillar to the snow and ice field on the right side (looking down). More rappels down the left side of the pillar below this snowfield led to a 45-degree gully on the right (looking down). This was down-climbed for approximately 500 feet, followed by one more rappel over the bergschrund back to the base of the route.

The first ascent party named this route in memory of Steve Mascioli, killed on Mount Hunter a few days before the first ascent of Mascioli's Pillar.

SOUTH BUTTRESS: RAMP ROUTE—ALASKA GRADE 3

This route has also been called the "Japanese Ramp." The South Buttress itself is one of the great ridges of Denali, extending for 12 miles from the South Peak, gradually turning west, and ending at the col to the east of Mount Frances (Peak, 10,450 feet). Technically speaking, it was first climbed in 1954 by Elton Thayer's party, approached from Ruth Glacier to the east (described in chapter 6). The Ramp Route is the route most often climbed on the South Buttress, and it was first climbed on July 3, 1965, over a period of fifteen days by Shiro Nishimae, Hisazumi Nakamura, and Masatsugu Kajiura, with the support of Yoshihito Tsukazaki, Katsuhiko Kaburagi, and Arthur Davidson. Of the three popular "South Face" routes (the other two are the West Rib and Cassin Ridge), it is generally considered less difficult than the West Rib, but it has considerable objective hazards. Aside from the dangers encountered on the East Fork of Kahiltna Glacier, the Ramp itself is swept by avalanches and falling ice, with numerous crevasses.

The Ramp is guarded by a major icefall from 10,000 to 12,000 feet. The icefall seems to change every season (in a few cases, it changed from day to day). The icefall has been bypassed on its left side, but this involves exposure to a dangerous hanging glacier. Some parties have climbed through the icefall, over steep seracs, before moving to the right, over and around crevasses, to a flat campsite at 12,000 feet at the bottom of the Ramp. But this site is potentially dangerous, as it is exposed to avalanches that may fall during storms. Ascend the 30- to 40-degree left side of the Ramp. There is a

South Buttress. BRIAN OKONEK, ALASKA-DENALI GUIDING

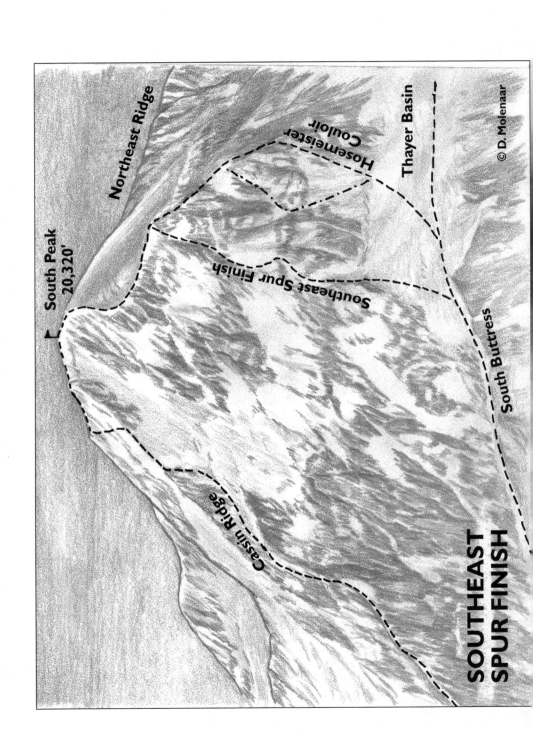

South Peak
20,320'

Northeast Ridge

Hosemeister Couloir

Thayer Basin

Southeast Spur Finish

South Buttress

Cassin Ridge

SOUTHEAST
SPUR FINISH

© D. Molenaar

campsite beneath some seracs at 14,800 feet. Continue up the left side of the Ramp to the crest of South Buttress at 15,600 feet, where it meets the Thayer Route. Follow the crest of the buttress northward, passing over Point 15,840 feet, to the two large snow basins (good campsites) beneath the Southeast Spur Finish of the South Peak of Denali.

The Southeast Spur Finish, also known as the "Upper Southeast Spur," was first climbed by Boyd Everett and Sam Cochrane during their climb of the complete Southeast Spur Route in 1962 (described in chapter 6). There is a large triangular face above the snow basin at 15,500 feet. Ascend the prominent snow couloir on the left side of the face. Cross the bergschrund at the base of this face on its right side, with a 45-degree slope immediately above. The couloir lessens to 35 to 40 degrees above 16,300 feet, but at 16,800 feet, it steepens to 45 degrees, and many parties go to the left and ascend easy rock along the ridge crest; this ridge is the eastern ridge of the south face. Continue up over mixed snow and rock to a good campsite at 17,800 feet, located beneath a rock band with a 50-degree snow couloir. Zigzag to the right of the couloir, mostly over snow, to 18,200 feet, where the upper part of the couloir is entered. This leads to a 35-degree snowfield that steepens to 50 degrees at 18,600 feet and then continues on to the summit ridge near Point 18,960 feet; the crux is just below the summit ridge, with 30 feet of 60- to 70-degree ice. Follow the ridge, traversing around the right side of Carter Horn (stay below 19,700 feet), to the summit of the South Peak.

It appears that most parties on the South Buttress descend it, rather than the Washburn Route.

Further reading: *AAJ* (1966): 119; *AAJ* (1968): 19–20; *ANAM* (1982): 28–29; *ANAM* (1985): 37; *ANAM* (1987): 25–26; *ANAM* (1993): 25–27; *ANAM* (1997): 8–9; Bill Dugovich, "Mount McKinley South Buttress Climb," *Summit* (July–August 1987): 1–8.

RIB VARIATION—ALASKA GRADE 3

This is also known as the "Wyoming Rib." It ascends the broad rib to the right of the Ramp. Although it is slightly more difficult than the Ramp, it has fewer objective dangers, as it is not as exposed to falling seracs and avalanches. It was first climbed in May 1988 by Andy Carson, Chuck Krago, Bill Alexander, Zach Etheridge, and John Chaklos. It leaves the Ramp Route at 12,000 feet and climbs the steep spur at the bottom of the Rib. The first ascent party camped beneath a large serac at 14,500 feet. A band of seracs at 15,000 feet is encountered before moving onto the crest of the South Buttress.

Further reading: *AAJ* (1989): 135-37.

SOUTH BUTTRESS: COMPLETE—ALASKA GRADE 3

The entire 12-mile South Buttress was climbed in May 1994 by Ron Bauer, Mark Asprey, Tahoe Rowland, Marcus Brown, Tom Whalen, and Mike Vanderbeek. They climbed onto the crest of the buttress from Kahiltna Base and took three weeks to complete the climb.

Further reading: *AAJ* (1995): 134.

· CHAPTER 6 ·

Southeastern Routes

This is the loneliest side of Denali. Fewer expeditions attempt Denali from this side than from any other, including the long northern approaches. Airdrops and airplane landings are prohibited within the Denali Wilderness, but the wilderness boundary on this side of Denali leaves large parts of the Northwest and West Forks of Ruth Glacier open to use by aircraft. At first glance, Ruth Glacier may appear to have the shortest approaches to climbing routes, but the variable snow surfaces, especially in mid- to late season (June and July), make aircraft landings on the upper Ruth Glacier risky propositions. Accounts of expeditions approaching Denali from the southeast are replete with tales of damaged aircraft.

The best landing site is at the late Don Sheldon's Mountain House, located approximately 1 mile west-northwest of Mount Barrille; the site is immediately west of the 5,710-foot benchmark shown on Bradford Washburn's map. This is approximately 4 miles from the junction of the Northwest and West Forks of Ruth Glacier. The next best landing site is near 7,000 feet along the West Fork of Ruth Glacier, beneath the north side of Mount Huntington; this site offers a downhill approach to the Northwest Fork of Ruth Glacier. The third choice is at the 7,700-foot level of the Northwest Fork of Ruth Glacier, between the East Buttress and the Southeast Spur, but this site may be dubious. The point is that approaches to this side of Denali may be longer than anticipated.

MARGARET PASS—ALASKA GRADE 2

Ruth Gap leads between Kahiltna and Ruth Glaciers, but it is a difficult route and, to the best of my knowledge, has never been traversed. An easier route (but exposed to avalanches on both its southeast and northwest sides)

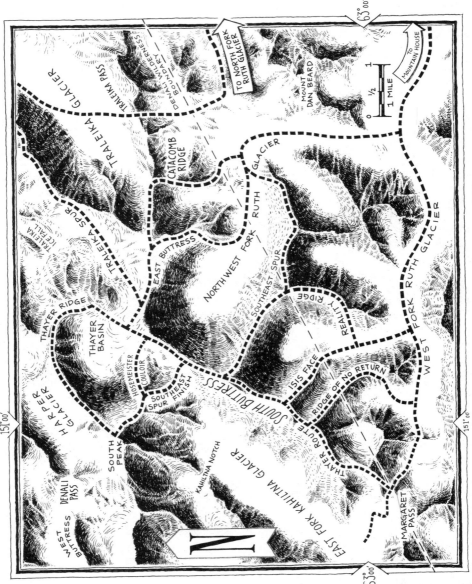

SOUTHEASTERN ROUTES

TRALEIKA GLACIER
TRALEIKA PASS
DENALI WILDERNESS BOUNDARY
TO NORTH FORK RUTH GLACIER
63° 00'
TO MOUNTAIN HOUSE
MOUNT DAN BEARD
½   1
1 MILE
0   1
CATACOMB RIDGE
RUTH GLACIER
NORTHWEST FORK RUTH
TRALEIKA SPUR
TRALEIKA ICEFALL
EAST BUTTRESS
SOUTHEAST SPUR
THAYER RIDGE
THAYER BASIN
REALITY RIDGE
WEST FORK RUTH GLACIER
HARPER GLACIER
HOSEMEISTER COULOIR
SOUTHEAST SPUR FINISH
SOUTH BUTTRESS
ISIS FACE
RIDGE OF NO RETURN
THAYER ROUTE
SOUTH PEAK
151° 00'
151° 00'
DENALI PASS
WEST BUTTRESS
KAHILTNA NOTCH
EAST FORK KAHILTNA GLACIER
MARGARET PASS
63° 00'

N

crosses the South Buttress to the north of Ruth Gap, leading from the West Fork of Ruth Glacier to the East Fork of Kahiltna Glacier. The first crossing was on June 20, 1963, by Jeff Duenwald, Jim Richardson, and Margaret Young, but this is also the route followed by Elton Thayer's 1954 South Buttress expedition. Ascend the West Fork of Ruth Glacier from the landing site north of Mount Huntington (which may have to be approached from the Mountain House, 8 miles distant). Pass through the icefall at 9,000 feet on its right side; the enormous crevasses near the head of the glacier at 9,500 feet are also negotiated to the right. The headwall that looms overhead is crossed by numerous open crevasses, studded with hanging seracs. Ascend the 45-degree right-hand side of the headwall, and traverse to the left, up and across a 60-degree slope. The angle eases back to 35 to 45 degrees near its top and leads to the broad crest of the South Buttress at 11,800 feet.

The west side of Margaret Pass is more gentle than its east side, but several ice cliffs bar the way at approximately 11,200 feet. Head west from the top of the pass and descend to the cliffs. With luck, a passage may be found; otherwise, rappels will be necessary. The rest of this slope is descended to the northwest, with many detours around crevasses and seracs, to the East Fork of Kahiltna Glacier.

Further reading: *AAJ* (1964): 52–53; *AAJ* (1979): 105–17; *ANAM* (1985): 32–34; *ANAM* (1996): 22–24; Lewis Leonard, "South of Denali: A Cross-Country Ski Tour," *Summit* (July–August 1981): 18–23, 26–27.

SOUTH BUTTRESS: THAYER ROUTE—ALASKA GRADE 3

This has also been called the "1954 Route." The Thayer Route climbs onto the crest of the South Buttress from the West Fork of Ruth Glacier via Margaret Pass and follows its crest to the bottom of the Southeast Spur Finish. Instead of following this to the summit, it crosses Thayer Basin and climbs to the summit of the South Peak via its northeast ridge. This long route was first climbed by George Argus, Leslie Viereck, Morton Wood, and Elton Thayer on May 12, 1954, over a period of eighteen days from the West Fork of Ruth Glacier; this does not include the eight days they spent approaching the mountain from Curry along the Alaska Railroad, 50 miles away.

From the top of Margaret Pass, head northeast and traverse the northwest side of Point 13,050 feet on a conveniently located bench to the saddle between this point and the main ridge of the South Buttress. The "Lotsa Face" looms above; 1,200 feet of 45-degree snow and ice leads up to the crest of the South Buttress at 13,790 feet. The ridge from here to Point 15,000 feet is usually corniced; the first ascent party was able to bypass Point 15,000 feet by traversing along the "tube" of an ice cornice that extended 60 to

80 feet to the west from the summit of this point. Soon a short 60-degree section is traversed across the west side of the ridge crest. Continue following the crest of the South Buttress, passing over Points 15,885 feet and 15,840 feet, to the base of the Southeast Spur Finish.

The Southeast Spur Finish is the logical conclusion to any of the routes on the South Buttress. This is described in chapter 5 under the South Buttress: Ramp Route. The Thayer party descended 1,500 feet to what is now called Thayer Basin. They then climbed the 30-degree couloir leading to the small notch just north of Point 15,720 feet. Thayer Ridge goes north from this notch, leading circuitously up to the northeast ridge of the South Peak. Scramble over and around giant granite blocks along the ridge, followed by a 1,000-foot, 30-degree snow slope to the top of Point 17,425 feet. Descend the rocky west ridge of Point 17,425 feet to the col at 17,200 feet, and follow the Parker-Browne Variation of the Muldrow Route to the summit of the South Peak.

Further reading: *AAJ* (1955): 51–69; *Harvard Mountaineering* 23 (January 1989): 87–96.

RIDGE OF NO RETURN—ALASKA GRADE 5

This 6,000-foot, 2-mile-long curved ridge leads from the West Fork of Ruth Glacier to Point 15,000 feet along Denali's South Buttress. The crest of this ridge is very narrow and at a relative low angle. This is the source of the route's name: Diagonal rappels are impossible, and in the event of retreat, every step must be down-climbed. It was first climbed on May 11, 1984, over a period of thirteen days by Renato Casarotto, solo. The route starts by ascending the left side of the west face of Point 10,170 feet. A triangular snow and ice face leads to an ice headwall that ends atop the ridge crest. The next 1,600 feet of vertical gain along the ridge can be summarized: enormous floating cornices, bypassed or overcome by climbing or traversing vertical and/or overhanging snow and ice with some rock towers (UIAA V). The ridge eventually merges into the southeast face of Point 15,000 feet. This begins with a snow and ice face, includes a mixed wall, and ends with more snow and ice; the steepest angle encountered in this section is 65 degrees. Casarotto descended the South Buttress from Point 15,000 feet.

Further reading: *AAJ* (1985):172–74.

ISIS FACE—ALASKA GRADE 5

This route ascends the southeast face of Point 15,430 feet along the South Buttress, following an aesthetic snow and ice arête. It gains over 7,000 feet in a little more than a mile. The Isis Face was first climbed over a period of eight days in May 1982 by Dave Stutzman and Jack Tackle. The route starts by ascending the hanging glacier to the right of the arête to a couloir that leads up and left. Climb the couloir to the crest of the fluted ridge. Follow the sides of the ridge upward; the first ascent party was forced to climb along the sides of the arête with loose snow over 50- to 60-degree water ice. Eventually, a long traverse to the left leads to a couloir. This ice couloir is narrow at first and then widens out, leading to the first rock band. This is overcome with YDS 5.8 and easy aid climbing. Climb onto the snow ridge above, and follow it to the second rock band. The technical crux of the route is here: passing a chockstone in a chimney with a pitch of overhanging ice. Relatively easy snow slopes then lead to the crest of the South Buttress.

Further reading: *ANAM* (1980): 18–19; *AAJ* (1983): plates 55–56.

REALITY RIDGE—ALASKA GRADE 4

This route ascends the south fork of the Southeast Spur. It gains 5,200 feet over a linear distance of 2 miles, meeting the main crest of the Southeast Spur atop Point 13,100 feet. It was first climbed over a period of thirty-seven days by Angus Thuermer (the only member to reach the summit on July 24, 1975), with support from Lincoln Stoller, Henry Florschutz, and Peter Metcalf. Metcalf made the second ascent with Glenn Randall in May 1982 in only nine days, summiting via the Southeast Spur Finish. The route begins from the 7,900-foot level of the cirque that is north of the West Fork of Ruth Glacier, bounded on the west by the Ridge of No Return and containing the Isis Face. Climb the west face of Point 10,370 feet, over steep snow mixed with easy rock and some small ice gullies, to the crest of Reality Ridge. Follow the ridge crest north, passing over Point 10,370 feet, to a small col surrounded by "meringue" cornices. Leave the col by traversing across the right (east) side of the ridge, passing underneath cornices, and then climb back onto the knife-edge ridge crest. Continue north, and an impasse on the right side leads to a short traverse across the left (west) side of the ridge, followed shortly by another traverse across the 45- to 50-degree east side of the ridge. This travers-ing eventually leads to a tight notch at the base of a rock wall at 10,800 feet.

Rappel out of the notch on its left (west) side down an ice gully. (The second ascent party climbed straight up the rock with a couple of aid moves to the crest of the ridge.) Next, diagonally ascend a rock face that leads to a gradually steepening 300-foot runnel; the first ascent party found this to be hard ice overlain with snow. The runnel ends with 75-degree ice just below the ridge crest. A short descent along the crest leads to a small col at 11,100 feet.

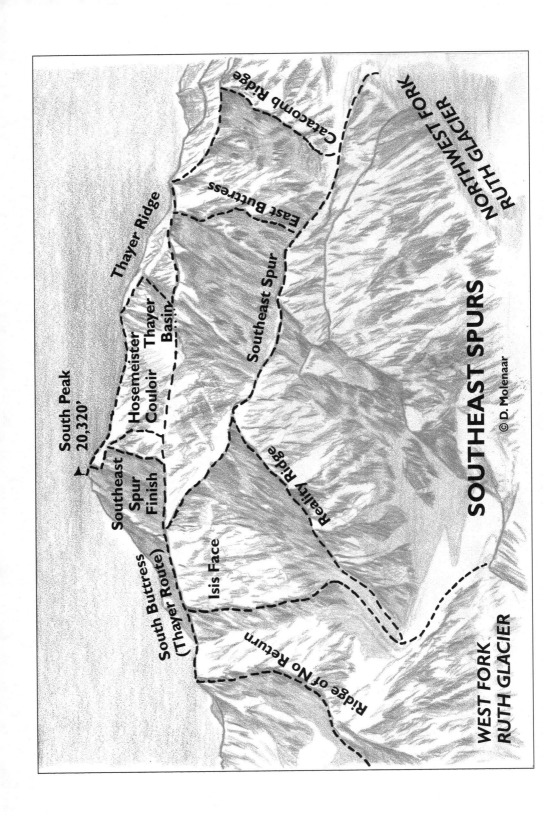

SOUTHEAST SPURS

©D. Molenaar

Catacomb Ridge

NORTHWEST FORK
RUTH GLACIER

East Buttress

Thayer Ridge

Thayer Basin

Hosemeister Couloir

Southeast Spur

South Peak
20,320'

Southeast Spur Finish

Reality Ridge

South Buttress
(Thayer Route)

Isis Face

Ridge of No Return

WEST FORK
RUTH GLACIER

The route continues by climbing up and across the east side of the ridge, passing immediately beneath cornices along the crest, to the top of a glacier that overhangs the east side of the ridge at 12,200 feet. Keep to the left (west) side of the ridge to the top of the Southeast Spur; most of this consists of moderate ice covered with snow, with the exception of a short vertical pitch of honeycombed snow. Continue up the Southeast Spur (described immediately below) to the summit. The first ascent party ascended Thayer Ridge, crossed Denali Pass, and descended via the Washburn Route.

Further reading: *AAJ* (1976): 313–19; Peter Metcalf, "Mt. McKinley Triple Indirect: 42 Days and a New Route on Denali," *Summit* (October 1976): 2–7, 39–41.

SOUTHEAST SPUR—ALASKA GRADE 4

This 12-mile-long ridge gains more than 12,000 feet, rising from the Northwest Fork of Ruth Glacier to the summit of the South Peak. It was first climbed over a period of twenty days by Boyd Everett and Sam Cochrane, with support from Hank Abrons, Charles Hollister, Sam Silverstein, and Chris Wren, and was summited on June 29, 1962. From the landing site at 7,700 feet on the Northwest Fork of Ruth Glacier (which may have to be approached from the Mountain House or the site along the West Fork of Ruth

Southeast Spurs. Brian Okonek, Alaska-Denali Guiding

Glacier at 7,000 feet, both approximately 9 miles away), head southeast before turning left and climb onto the face that leads up to the ridge. Climb the 30- to 45-degree face directly to 8,500 feet and then traverse diagonally to the right to the base of a large ice wall at 9,000 feet. Bypass this by traversing to the left, and climb onto the ridge crest. The first ascent party placed a camp above this ice wall at 9,200 feet. Traverse up and right across a 55-degree face to the prominent 100-foot ice wall at 9,700 feet. Traverse to the right along the base of this wall, and pass it on its far right-hand side. A 40-degree and then a 50-degree pitch lead straight up a potential avalanche slope, followed by a 300-foot traverse to the left that ends at the base of a serac. Two more pitches straight up end at a nearly level platform to the right of The Arrow—a 200 foot vertical ice ridge topped by huge overhanging cornices. This was overcome by going to the right from the platform and climbing a 65-degree slope underneath a cornice with a 10-foot overhang, then going up and left to a smaller cornice, which was tunneled through to the crest of the spur.

The next six pitches ascend a series of cornices and strange hidden crevasses, apparently covering the gaps between the rock towers along the spur. The south side of the spur, beneath the cornices, is 45 to 50 degrees steep. Ice climbing was not as advanced in 1962 as it is today, and the first ascent party was forced to follow the narrow strip between the hard blue ice below and the easier soft snow of the cornices above. The last pitch of this section goes left for 50 feet across one of these strange hidden crevasses and then climbs a vertical to overhanging 20-foot ice wall, overcome by using aid off a picket. A 45- to 65-degree slope then leads for two short pitches to the right-hand side of a 100-foot ice wall, the Corner. The traverse around the Corner is the crux of the route. Go to the left across this 65-degree slope with rotten snow over ice, and climb through more airy snow to the top of the Corner at 10,800 feet.

Easy climbing leads for half a mile to the top of Point 11,280 feet and continues another half mile along the crest to the base of the Fluting. This is a section of knife-edged ridge about 1,000 feet long with fluted ice faces on both its sides. The first ascent party traversed the north face of the Fluting, keeping 200 feet beneath the ridge crest, exposed to overhanging cornices. This involved climbing a 15-foot overhanging bergschrund, followed by six pitches zigzagging up a 55-degree slope. (In retrospect, Boyd Everett believed that the route should have been atop the corniced crest. Falling through a cornice is not as bad as having a cornice fall down on a climber.) Above the Fluting, the route goes to the right, traverses through a field of seracs, and passes a 300-foot east-facing ice wall on its right side. A short serac barrier crosses the entire ridge above the ice wall. This is overcome by means of a pitch up 50-degree ice. The slope above averages 30 degrees and leads to the top of Point 13,100 feet.

Continue along the crest of the Southeast Spur, skirting and passing over a small vertical ice wall on its left side below 12,900 feet, along the way to the 12,700-foot saddle. Above the saddle, the route to the South Buttress is 30 degrees in angle for the most part, with the exception of a 45-degree stretch between 13,900 and 14,100 feet. It then goes straight up to the 15,000-foot level, where it makes a diagonal ascent to the right through a large couloir to meet the crest of the South Buttress at 15,700 feet. The first ascent party summited via the Southeast Spur Finish, described in chapter 5 under the South Buttress: Ramp Route.

Further reading: *AAJ* (1962): 49–52; *AAJ* (1963): 381–89; *Harvard Mountaineering* 16 (May 1963): 22–36; Chris Wren, "We Climbed Our Highest Mountain," *Look* (October 9, 1962): 60–69; Boyd Everett, *1962 Southeast Spur Mt. McKinley Expedition*, mimeographed expedition report, available at the Talkeetna Ranger Station.

EAST BUTTRESS—ALASKA GRADE 3

This route was first climbed May 24, 1963, by Peter Lev, Rod Newcomb, and Al Read, with support from Warren Bleser, Fred Wright, and Jed Williamson. (These last three climbers were stopped less than 300 feet from the summit by wind and whiteout.) It took a total of twenty-four days to summit from the base of the route, not counting the twelve-day approach from the landing site, located near the present site of the Mountain House in the Don Sheldon Amphitheater. The approach is over the Northwest Fork of Ruth Glacier, which is exposed to potential massive avalanches in its higher reaches from the Southeast Spur and the upper South Buttress. The first ascent party eventually established its base camp at 9,100 feet at the very bottom of the route, slightly above the glacier, for protection from avalanches from the east face of the South Buttress.

The route itself ascends a system of ramps and gullies that are exposed to avalanches between 9,300 and 11,800 feet, and extreme caution must be exercised during the ascent. The best route varies from year to year between 11,800 and 13,200 feet, where it passes through a complex series of icefalls, steep snow, and crevasses. The campsites at 11,400, 12,400, and 13,700 feet are safe. The climbing starts with the Bulge, a 450-foot, 45-degree convex slope, which consisted of windslab over soft snow at the time of the first ascent. It continues up 30- to 40-degree slopes before making a steep traverse to the right to a campsite near a bergschrund at 11,400 feet, beneath a prominent ridge. The first ascent party attempted this ridge, to avoid avalanches, but finally abandoned it and ascended the gully leading up and left from the camp. This leads to a 150-foot, 70-degree ice wall (the crux of the route) at 11,800 feet, near the top of the gully. From the top of the ice wall, the route goes up and left for several hundred yards to a campsite at 12,400 feet, located on top of a slight ridge.

The route traverses several hundred yards to the east before going straight up for 800 feet to the base of an overhanging, 40-foot ice cliff. The first ascent party overcame this by climbing an ice block that had separated from the top of the cliff, but this was not a permanent feature, and subsequent parties have climbed through seracs and ice cliffs with angles up to 80 degrees. Continue climbing to the base of the rock wall above; there is a potential campsite in the bergschrund at the base of this wall at 13,700 feet. The route then goes to the left and ascends 50- to 55-degree ice ramps next to the rock. The first ascent party climbed 800 feet to a knife-edged ridge, which they followed to the plateau beneath Point 14,630 feet; subsequent parties have climbed the 45-degree slope above directly to the plateau. Go west along the level top of the East Buttress for approximately 1 mile, and traverse across and down the north face of Point 14,730 feet to the 13,800-foot level of Thayer Basin. The first ascent party summited via Thayer Ridge and descended the East Buttress.

Further reading: *AAJ* (1963): 453–60; *AAJ* (1964): 37–42; *ANAM* (1982): 19–21; *ANAM* (1983): 32; *Appalachia* (June 1964): 64–75; Warren Bleser, "McKinley's East Buttress," *Summit* (September 1965): 12–15; Rick Meinig, "Denali East Buttress Ascent," *Summit* (December 1977): 2–7; *1963 East Buttress Mt. Denali Expedition*, mimeographed expedition report available from the Talkeetna Ranger Station.

BELL VARIATION—ALASKA GRADE 3

This variation has less objective hazards than the 1963 route, avoiding the icefalls and crevasses between 11,800 and 13,200 feet. It was climbed by Joe Terravecchia, Scott Hartle, and George Bell, Jr., in June 1986. After landing at 7,700 feet on the Northwest Fork of Ruth Glacier, they ascended the ramp system to the base of the first ice wall at 11,800 feet, where they camped in a bergschrund. Traverse to the right and climb a moderate 50-degree ice couloir for six pitches to the top of the ridge, meeting it at a prominent pinnacle. After following the corniced ridge for approximately two pitches, a traverse to the left leads back to easier terrain and the East Buttress route, meeting it above the overhanging ice wall at 13,200 feet. The first ascent party continued to the summit via the Southeast Spur Finish and descended the South Buttress Ramp Route.

Further reading: *AAJ* (1987): 147–49.

CATACOMB RIDGE—ALASKA GRADE 4

This sharp ridge leads from the Northwest Fork of Ruth Glacier onto the East Buttress of Denali, meeting it at Point 11,920 feet. Catacomb Ridge is cut by crevasses and cornices, with shafts and cavities across and along its crest and networks of holes beneath each campsite; the first ascent party found a large steel shovel to be an essential piece of equipment. The campsites are good, however: large and flat, and free of danger from rockfalls and avalanches. The ridge was first climbed over twenty-one days by Joe Davidson, Gus Benner, Ken Jones, Niels Andersen, Bob Fries, Jim Given, and Peter Reagan, summiting on July 2, 1969. This party landed near the Mountain House and spent a week approaching the base of the route and scouting approaches onto the East Buttress. They eventually selected Catacomb Ridge, marked by four rocks on its crest when viewed from the southeast. The route starts from Ruth Glacier by ascending a steep snow slope immediately east of the lowest rock on the ridge. Climb the 45-degree slope (black ice covered with snow) for three pitches to the Second Rock, and then traverse left to Andersen's Creek, a three-pitch ice gully that leads between the First Rock and the Second Rock. A short waterfall (literally, during warm temperatures) pitch leads to the crest of the ridge. Climb the broad ridge crest, passing the Second Rock on its west side by means of a 60-degree ice pitch, and continue following the broad crest over alternating stretches of ice and snow to 9,200 feet, where there is a campsite just beneath the monolithic Third Rock.

The ridge becomes a sharp, weaving knife-edge immediately below the Third Rock. Climb the ridge and then traverse the Third Rock on its west side over a series of narrow, exposed ledges. These lead to a 60-degree ice pitch that ends on top of a very sharp, slightly corniced knife-edge ridge. Follow the ridge to a steep snow slope with a large crevasse that cuts completely across the ridge. The first ascent party found a rickety bridge across this crevasse that led to the base of the Fourth Rock. Climb the Fourth Rock directly over mixed snow and rock. This is followed by the Serac Traverse, passing beneath a terrifying corniced ridge; it is three pitches long across easy rock, followed by slopes of 60 to 75 degrees and ending at another broad section. Next is the Haunted Traverse, which leads up and across the east side of the ridge for five pitches over 50- to 55-degree hard ice covered with snow; it is exposed to falling ice, and there are many creaking, popping, and groaning crevasses. It ends at Lunch Rocks, an obvious outcrop. Go straight up from Lunch Rocks, over a steep black-ice cliff, to regain the ridge crest at 10,600 feet. The first ascent party placed a camp here and discovered a large crevasse that ran along the crest of the ridge (as opposed to across the ridge). Continue up the crest of the ridge to the Matterhorn Cornice, which is passed on its east side, followed by an ice step; the lower part of the ice step is 60 degrees, but the upper part is vertical black ice. Continue up the ridge to Point 11,920 feet.

Go west along the East Buttress from Point 11,920 feet. This starts out wide and flat and then abruptly meets the Cornice Traverse. The traverse across these floating cornices consists of three pitches of very steep (up to 60-degree snow, with some ice), difficult climbing. This ends at a 300-foot flat section, followed by the Giant Step, a 100-foot vertical ice cliff, which is climbed directly. Next is a long plateau, and then a series of four large alternating cornices, dubbed "Fairyland" by the first ascent party. Fairyland ends at an ice cliff, the bottom of a small hanging glacier. Climb to the top of the cliff. The 2,500-foot face above is 45 degrees, snow with patches of black ice, split by a bergschrund halfway up. This leads to the large 14,000-foot plateau atop the East Buttress. Go west along the level top of the East Buttress for approximately 1 mile and traverse across and down the north face of Point 14,730 feet to the 13,800-foot level of Thayer Basin. The first ascent party continued to the summit via Thayer Ridge and descended Catacomb Ridge.

Further reading: *AAJ* (1963): 453–60; *AAJ* (1970): 63–67; Joseph K. Davidson, *The East Ridge of Mt. McKinley—1969: Expedition Report,* mimeographed, available from the Talkeetna Ranger Station.

Mention should be made of Dr. Frederick A. Cook's and Edward N. Barrill's alleged ascent of Denali in 1906. Supporters of Dr. Cook believe that he and Barrill ascended the East Buttress from Traleika Pass, followed Thayer Ridge, and climbed to the summit of the South Peak from September 11 through 16, 1906. Cook misspelled Barrill's name, and this error continues today as "Mt. Barrille" on the USGS and Washburn maps.

HOSEMEISTER COULOIR—ALASKA GRADE 3

This couloir is on the upper southeast face and was climbed on June 20, 1991, by Lee James and Bob Gammelin, after an approach from the Ramp Route on the South Buttress. Climb the right branch of the large couloir on the southeast face above Thayer Basin. This consists of 50- to 60-degree ice and snow, with some loose rock at the top of the couloir. There is a level campsite on the right edge of the couloir at 16,000 feet. From the top of the couloir, follow the ridge (the first ascent party also chopped out a campsite at approximately 18,000 feet) over Point 18,960 feet, and follow the Southeast Spur Finish to the summit. The first ascent party traversed to the right on the descent and went down the central branch of the large couloir to avoid the rock encountered during the ascent.

Further reading: *AAJ* (1962): 49–52; *AAJ* (1963): 453–60; *AAJ* (1992): 116–17.

TRALEIKA PASS—ALASKA GRADE 2

This pass leads between the Ruth and Traleika Glaciers. It is atop the East Buttress at 10,600 feet, approximately 1.2 miles west of the Traleika Col, which is marked on the Washburn and USGS maps. Its north and south sides were climbed by two separate expeditions in 1956, but it wasn't crossed until April 16–17, 1978, by Ned Gillette, Allan Bard, Doug Weins, and Galen Rowell. The 2,500-foot north side of the pass is steep, unconsolidated deep snow (with one 60-degree section). The 1,000-foot headwall on the south side is even steeper (average 70 degrees) and is descended by means of rappels and belays. Snow and ice bollards may be the only option for anchors, and the avalanche danger increases during the day due to the direct southern exposure of this face. Finally, a deep bergschrund must be crossed at the bottom of this face. The route continues down to the saddle northwest of Point 9,650 feet. The 1978 party descended the bumpy and snow-filled icefall to the east from this saddle and went down the North Fork of Ruth Glacier to the Don Sheldon Amphitheater. The 1956 Walter Gonnason party reached this saddle from the west, by climbing the icefall leading to it from the Northwest Fork of Ruth Glacier. The Catacomb Ridge Expedition in 1969 found this latter icefall to be too active for safe climbing.

Further reading: *AAJ* (1979): 105–17; *AAJ* (1957): 153–56; *AAJ* (1958): plate 18a; *AAJ* (1963): 453–60; *AAJ* (1970): 63–64.

• APPENDIX A •

Further Reading

INSTRUCTION

Mountaineering: Denali National Park and Preserve. Available from the Talkeetna Ranger Station and on the Internet at http://www.nps.gov/dena/mountain/talkeet.htm.

Randall, Glenn. *Mount McKinley Climber's Handbook.* Evergreen, CO: Chockstone Press, 1992. 118 pp. An excellent introduction to expedition climbing, with an emphasis on subarctic mountaineering as practiced on Denali.

HISTORY

Beckey, Fred. *Mount McKinley: Icy Crown of North America.* Seattle: The Mountaineers, 1993. 320 pp. Covers geology, early human history, and mountaineering history from the earliest surveyors to modern times. Includes descriptions of the West Buttress (Washburn), the West Rib, Muldrow Glacier, and Cassin Ridge and a discussion of logistics for current expeditions.

Moore, Terris. *Mt. McKinley: The Pioneer Climbs.* Seattle: The Mountaineers, 1981. 203 pp. Exploration, attempts, and ascents of Denali to 1942.

Washburn, Bradford, and David Roberts. *Mount McKinley: The Conquest of Denali.* New York: Harry N. Abrams, 1991. 240 pp. History of climbs, with many photographs.

Waterman, Jonathan. *High Alaska: A Historical Guide to Denali, Mount Foraker and Mount Hunter.* Golden, CO: American Alpine Club, 1988. 398 pp. Describes the history of all the routes established on the high peaks of

Denali National Park and Preserve, with many Bradford Washburn photographs.

Waterman, Jonathan. *Surviving Denali: A Study of Accidents on Mt. McKinley, 1910–1990.* 2d ed. Golden, CO: American Alpine Club, 1991. 264 pp. This is an excellent analysis of accidents on Denali.

Addresses

CLIMBING REGISTRATION

Denali National Park and Preserve
Talkeetna Ranger Station
P.O. Box 588
Talkeetna, AK 99676
    Telephone: 907-733-2231
    Fax: 907-733-1465
    E-mail: DENA_Talkeetna_office@nps.gov
    Web site: http://www.nps.gov/dena/mountain/talkeet.htm

TRANSPORTATION FROM ANCHORAGE
TO TALKEETNA OR DENALI PARK

Denali Overland Transportation Company
P.O. Box 330
Talkeetna, AK 99676
    Telephone: 907-733-2384
    Fax: 907-733-2385

Talkeetna Shuttle Service
P.O. Box 468
Talkeetna, AK 99676
    Telephone: 907-733-1725
    Toll-free: 888-288-6008
    Fax: 907-733-2222
    E-mail: tshuttle@alaska.net

Alaska Backpacker Shuttle
P.O. Box 232493
Anchorage, AK 99523-2493
    Telephone: 907-344-8775
    Toll-free: 800-266-8625
    Fax: 907-522-7382
    E-mail: abst@juno.com

The Alaska Railroad
Passenger Services
P.O. Box 107500
Anchorage, AK 99510-7500
    Telephone: 907-265-2494
    From outside Alaska: 800-544-0552
    Fax: 907-265-2323

AIR TAXIS

Alpine Air, Inc.
P.O. Box 1047
Girdwood, AK 99587
    Telephone: 907-783-2360
    Fax: 907-754-1504
    E-mail: alpinair@alaska.net
    Web site: http://www.alaska.net/~alpinair

Doug Geeting Aviation
P.O. Box 42
Talkeetna, AK 99676
    Telephone: 907-733-2366
    Toll-free: 800-770-2366
    Fax: 907-733-1000
    E-mail: airtours@alaska.net
    Web site: http://www.alaska.net/~airtours/

Hudson Air Service
P.O. Box 648
Talkeetna, AK 99676
    Telephone: 907-733-2321
    Toll-free: 800-478-2321
    Fax: 907-733-2333

E-mail: hasi@customcpu.com
Web site: http://www.alaskan.com/hudsonair

K2 Aviation
P.O. Box 545
Talkeetna, AK 99676
    Telephone: 907-733-2291
    Toll-free: 800-764-2291
    Fax: 907-733-1221
    E-mail: flyk2@alaska.net
    Web site: http://www.alaska.net/~flyk2/

Max Schwab Airlines
P.O. Box 295
Talkeetna, AK 99676
    Telephone: 907-733-2681
    Fax: 907-733-1353

McKinley Air Service
P.O. Box 544
Talkeetna, AK 99676
    Telephone: 907-733-1765
    Toll-free: 800-564-1765
    Fax: 907-733-1965
    E-mail: mckair@alaska.net
    Web site: http://www.alaska.net/~mckair/

Spotted Dog Aviation
3072 N. Circle
Anchorage, AK 99507
    Telephone and fax: 907-344-3249
    E-mail: spotdog@arctic.net

Talkeetna Air Taxi
P.O. Box 73
Talkeetna, AK 99676
    Telephone: 907-733-2218
    Toll-free: 800-533-2219
    Fax: 907-733-1434
    E-mail: flytat@alaska.net
    Web site: http://www.alaska.net/~flytat/

DOG SLEDS

Denali Dog Tours and Wilderness Enterprises
P.O. Box 378
Healy, AK 99743
    Telephone: 907-683-2644

GUIDE SERVICES

Alaska-Denali Guiding, Inc.
P.O. Box 566
Talkeetna, AK 99676
    Telephone: 907-733-2649
    Fax: 907-733-1362
    E-mail: adg@alaska.net

American Alpine Institute, Ltd.
1212 24th Street
Bellingham, WA 98225
    Telephone: 206-671-1505

Fantasy Ridge Mountain Guides
P.O. Box 1679
Telluride, CO 81435
    Telephone or fax: 303-728-3546

Mountain Trip
P.O. Box 91161
Anchorage, AK 99509
    Telephone: 907-345-6499

National Outdoor Leadership School
P.O. Box AA
Lander, WY 82502
    Telephone: 307-332-6973

Rainier Mountaineering, Inc.
535 Dock Street, Suite 209
Tacoma, WA 98402
    Telephone: 206-627-6242
    Fax: 206-569-2227

· APPENDIX C ·

Equipment List

CLOTHING

overboots
plastic double boots
cold-weather socks with liners
    (three pairs)
plastic bags (as vapor barrier liners
    for socks)
lightweight long underwear, tops
    and bottoms
"expedition-weight" long under-
    wear, tops and bottoms
pile sweater
pile jacket
pile trousers
pile balaclava

windbreaker
windpants
synthetic or down parka with hood
warm cap
neck gaiter
balaclava
face mask
glove liners
wool mittens
overmitts
gaiters
sun hat
dark glasses
bandanna

CAMPING EQUIPMENT

knapsack
duffel bag
straps
sunscreen
lip balm
water bottles
compass
altimeter

thermometer
pocketknife
first-aid kit
four-season tent
snow shovel
snow saw
sleeping bag, rated to –20° F
    minimum

vapor barrier liner for sleeping bag
two foam pads
sleeping bag cover
cup and spoon
cigarette lighters
stove, windshield, and platform

fuel bottles
cooking pots
toilet paper
heavy-duty garbage bags
long pole

CLIMBING EQUIPMENT

snowshoes or skis with climbing
    skins
ski poles
sled
wands
ice ax
crampons
prusiks
ascenders
50 meters of 9-mm climbing rope
another short rope for crevasse
    rescue
seat and chest harnesses

ice screws, pickets, and/or
    deadmen
pulleys
carabiners
runners

In addition, for technical routes:
ice hammer
helmet
chocks
rock pitons
aiders

OTHER

radio with extra batteries
repair kit
toothbrush, toothpaste, soap
notebooks, pens, pencils

topo maps
books
camera and film

And don't forget the food and stove fuel!

• ABOUT THE AUTHOR •

R. J. Secor has twenty-eight years of mountaineering experience and has been hiking and skiing since he learned how to walk. An enthusiastic peak bagger, he has climbed 280 different peaks for a total of 584 summits in the High Sierra of California, in addition to extensive climbing in Baja California, Arizona, Nevada, Utah, Idaho, Washington, Oregon, Wyoming, Montana, British Columbia, Alberta, and Alaska. Other mountain adventures have taken him as far afield as the Himalaya in Tibet and Nepal, the Karakoram in Pakistan, the Andes in Argentina, and the volcanoes of Mexico. His other books are *The High Sierra: Peaks, Passes, and Trails, Mexico's Volcanoes: A Climbing Guide,* and *Aconcagua: A Climbing Guide.* He is a member of the Sierra Club, the American Alpine Club, the Southern California Mountaineers Association, and the California Mountaineering Club.

• ABOUT THE ILLUSTRATORS •

Dee Molenaar is a former summit guide and park ranger in Mount Rainier National Park and has been mountaineering for more than fifty years, including such mountains as K2, Mount St. Elias, and Mount Kennedy. He is noted for his mountain watercolors, sketches, and maps, which have appeared in many books and exhibits. He lives in Burley, Washington.

Mike Clelland is an instructor for the National Outdoor Leadership School and illustrator for *Climbing.* He has illustrated eleven climbing and camping books, including *Knots and Ropes for Climbers* and *NOLS Cookery.* He lives in Driggs, Idaho.

· INDEX ·